THE SEARCH FOR SIGNIFICANCE

RAPHA RESOURCES INCLUDE...

THE SEARCH FOR SIGNIFICANCE (Book)
Robert S. McGee

THE SEARCH FOR SIGNIFICANCE
(Book and Workbook Combined)
Robert S. McGee

THE SEARCH FOR SIGNIFICANCE
SMALL GROUP LEADER'S GUIDE(Booklet)
Robert S. McGee

THE SEARCH FOR SIGNIFICANCE
4-Part Video Seminar with Study Guide & Promotion Kit
Robert S. McGee

THE SEARCH FOR SIGNIFICANCE
(Youth Discussion Manual)
Robert S. McGee & Dawson McAllister

DISCIPLINE WITH LOVE (Book)
Robert S. McGee

RAPHA'S 12-STEP PROGRAM FOR OVERCOMING
CHEMICAL DEPENDENCY (Workbook)
Robert S. McGee, Pat Springle, Susan Joiner

THE PARENT FACTOR (Book)
Robert S. McGee, Pat Springle, Jim Craddock

CODEPENDENCY (Book and Workbook)
Pat Springle

CODEPENDENCY SMALL GROUP
LEADER'S GUIDE(Booklet)
Pat Springle

DRUG FREE FOR GOOD
4-Phase Christian Recovery & Family
Education/Training Program

THE SEARCH FOR SIGNIFICANCE
BOOK

Robert S. McGee

Second Edition

Rapha
PUBLISHING

Houston, Texas

The Search for Significance

First Printing, Second Edition, 1990
Printed in the United States of America

ISBN: 0-945276-11-7

To my wife, Marilyn, who has given of herself so that I might minister these truths, both personally and now by the written word.

CONTENTS

Acknowledgments

The concepts presented in this book have been utilized at our counseling centers and seminars for many years. The results have been so phenomenal that we were compelled to produce this book.

Many have contributed to *The Search for Significance*. I want to especially thank my staff, whose great dedication to the spreading of these truths is immeasurable. I also want to thank Rick Hove, Ray Anderson, Melanie Ahlquist, Dan Hayes, Dr. Steve Spotts, Conrad Koch, Richard Price, Sandy Ballard, Jay Hamman, Becky Blount, and especially my mother, Minerva McGee, all of whom have made significant contributions to this book. Finally, I would like to thank Pat Springle and Susan Joiner, who were instrumental in bringing clarity and insight to this material.

Introduction

When Christ told His disciples, *You shall know the truth, and the truth shall make you free* (John 8:32), He was referring not only to an intellectual assent to the truth, but also to the application of truth in the most basic issues of life: our goals, our motives, and our sense of self-worth. Unfortunately, many of us give only lip-service to the powerful truths of the Scriptures without allowing them to affect the basis of our self-esteem in a radical way. Instead, we continue to seek our security and purpose from worldly sources: personal success, status, beauty, wealth, and the approval of others. These rewards may fulfill us for a short time, but they soon lead us to a sense of urgency to succeed and be approved again.

To meet these compelling needs, we drive ourselves to achieve, doing virtually anything to make people happy with us, and spend countless hours and dollars trying to look "just right." Often, we avoid situations and people where the risks of failure and rejection are high. It's a rat race that can't be won by simply running faster. We need to get off of this hopeless treadmill, and learn to apply the foundational truths that can motivate us to live for Christ rather than for the approval of other people.

Christ's death paid the penalty for our sins, and His resurrection gives us new life, new goals, and new hope. He has given us complete security and challenging purpose. These are not based on our abilities, but on His grace and the power of His Spirit. Yes, Christ wants us to be zealous and ambitious, but not about our success or status. If we understand His forgiveness and acceptance, we will pursue the right things—Christ and His cause—and we will be free to enjoy His love.

This is the revised and expanded version of *The Search for Significance*. The response from those who have read the book and used the workbook has been overwhelming. It is my prayer that the Lord will use these materials to convince you of His love, forgiveness, and purposes for your life.

> *For the love of Christ controls us, having concluded this,*
> *that one died for all, therefore all died;*
> *and He died for all, that they who live should no longer*
> *live for themselves, but for Him who died and rose again on*
> *their behalf.*
>
> 2 Cor. 5:14-15

THE SEARCH FOR SIGNIFICANCE

One
Turning on the Light

Tim Woodall is a young regional sales representative for a company that manufactures building materials. He travels by car, covering a large section of East Texas as he visits building supply stores in the many small towns there.

Almost a year ago, after his last appointment in the day, Tim decided to drive home instead of spending another night in a motel. At about midnight, driving down a lonely, two-lane country highway, he dozed off. His car ran off the road, hit an embankment, and flipped over.

Tim was dazed, and when he moved, seemed to hurt all over. He managed to struggle out of his car, and then lay on the grass trying to grasp what had happened to him. *I'm okay,* he kept telling himself. *It's really not that bad.*

About forty-five minutes later, Tim, barely conscious, heard the sound of an approaching car. He tried to raise himself up, but it was useless; he was too weak. The car zoomed past, and then braked. Bob and Natalie Johnson were driving through the night from El Paso, Texas, to Montgomery, Alabama, to visit their daughter. In the moonlight, Natalie had spotted the overturned car from the corner of her eye. Now, her husband backed down the road and pulled over onto the shoulder. Beyond their headlights, they could clearly see the wrecked car, and lying next to it, Tim.

1

Tim lay in a pool of blood. Beneath the light, the Johnsons discovered that his head and arm were badly cut, and as they tried to help him to his feet, realized that his left leg was probably fractured.

Seeing his own blood-stained shirt; the dirt, wet beside him; and the concern on the Johnsons' faces, Tim began to shake uncontrollably, suddenly aware that he was badly hurt. He was, in fact, slowly bleeding to death, but due to shock, wasn't fully able to comprehend the extent of his wounds.

The Johnsons lifted Tim into their car and sped him toward the county hospital, where his cuts were stitched and his fractured leg put into a splint. This would be replaced with a cast when the swelling went down.

If the Johnsons hadn't been driving to Alabama that night; if Natalie had been looking another way; if the headlights of their car hadn't enabled them to find Tim in the darkness, he might have died.

This story illustrates a reality in many of our lives: We are hurt, emotionally, relationally, and spiritually, but because we aren't aware of the extent of our wounds, we can't take steps toward healing and health. Our problem is not stupidity, but a lack of objectivity. Because of this, we fail to see the reality of pain, hurt, and anger in our lives.

A college student was considered "the life of the party." She was intelligent, witty, and sociable, but when she was alone, she experienced deep loneliness and seething resentment.

A businessman who, as a child, was neglected by his ambitious father thought, *If I can just get that promotion, then I'll be happy. Success is what really counts in life!* He got many promotions and raises because he was driven to perform well, but happiness continued to elude him.

A housewife with three children painfully wonders, *Why is it that I don't feel close to my husband?* Having grown up with an alcoholic father and a demanding mother, this woman has never felt lovable, and so isn't able to receive her husband's love.

An articulate pastor speaks powerfully about the unconditional love and grace of God, yet he is plagued by guilt. He is driven to succeed in his

2

public ministry, but is passive and withdrawn around his family. He has never understood how to apply his own teaching to *his* life and relationships.

We all have experienced the inability to be objective about our experiences, thoughts, and behavior in different circumstances. This objective "light" didn't begin to penetrate my own life until shortly after I had entered the business world. Before that time, whenever I felt the pain of rejection, the sting of sarcasm, or anything less than the complete approval of others, I tried to shrug it off. I reasoned that because of my status as a Christian, I should exude an attitude of happiness and contentment in all things. When something didn't go the way I'd hoped or planned it would, I simply told myself it didn't really matter. Though I was able to fool myself in these instances, my gloomy countenance told those who were closest to me another story.

On one such occasion, a good friend of mine inquired about what was wrong. "You seem troubled," he said. "Is anything bothering you?"

"Me? No, I'm fine."

"You don't seem fine to me," he persisted. "You're acting as though you might be depressed about something."

I stuck to my time-tested text. "No, really, I *am* fine. I guess I've just been a little pressured lately."

The truth was that an idea I'd presented in a business meeting the week before had been challenged and later, shot down. I didn't think it really mattered at first, but after hearing my friend's remarks, I began to wonder if I were being honest with myself.

Several weeks later, I phoned this friend to thank him for confronting me about my behavior. I briefly told him about the business meeting and said, "Realizing I was hurt because my idea was rejected has enabled me to be honest with the Lord about my feelings and begin working through them."

"I'm sorry about what happened," he said, "but I appreciate your honesty, and think it's great that you're doing something constructive with a difficult situation."

Over time, I began to confide in this friend about other problems I encountered. He helped me a great deal. At times, he would say, "Here's how I'd feel in your situation. I'd be angry because.... Do *you* feel angry?" Or, "I'd be hurt because.... Do *you* feel hurt?"

In the light of his honesty and love, and through the gracious work of the Holy Spirit, I began to be honest with myself and with God. The tough exterior I had developed started cracking, and I began to experience the pain I had neither wanted nor allowed myself to feel. This was hardly pleasant, but acknowledging the presence of hurt in my life was my first step toward finding comfort.

Why do some of us lack objectivity? Why can't we see the reality of our lives? Why are we afraid to "turn on the lights"?

There are a number of answers to these questions, and they vary for each person. Perhaps we think that our situations are "normal," that experiencing loneliness, hurt, and anger is really all there is to life. Perhaps we want to be "good Christians," and believing that *good* Christians don't have problems or feelings like ours, we deny the existence of our painful emotions. Perhaps our lack of objectivity is a learned response from childhood. All of us desperately want our parents to be loving and supportive. If ours aren't (or weren't), we may protect our concept of them by blaming ourselves for their lack of love, and deny that we have been hurt by their behavior.

Human beings develop elaborate defense mechanisms to block pain and gain significance. We suppress emotions; we are compulsive perfectionists; we drive ourselves to succeed, or withdraw and become passive; we attack people who hurt us; we punish ourselves when we fail; we try to say clever things to be accepted; we help people so that we will be appreciated; and we say and do countless other things.

A sense of need usually propels us to look for an alternative. We may have the courage to examine ourselves and may desperately want to change, but may be unsure of how and where to start. We may refuse to look honestly within for fear of what we'll find, or we may be afraid that even if we can discover what's wrong, nothing can help us.

It is difficult—if not impossible—to turn on the light of objectivity by ourselves. We need guidance from the Holy Spirit, as well as the honesty, love, and encouragement of at least one other person who's willing to help us. Even then, we may become depressed as we begin to discover the effects of our wounds. Some of us have deep emotional and spiritual scars resulting from the neglect, abuse, and manipulation that often accompany living in a dysfunctional family (alcoholism, drug abuse, divorce, absent father or mother, excessive anger, verbal and/or physical abuse, etc.), but all of us bear the effects of our own sinful nature and the imperfections of others.

Whether your hurts are deep or relatively mild, it is wise to be honest about them in the context of affirming relationships so that healing can begin.

Many of us mistakenly believe that God doesn't want us to be honest about our lives. We think that He will be upset with us if we tell Him how we really feel. But the Scriptures tell us that God does not want us to be superficial—in our relationship with Him, with others, or in our own lives. David wrote, *Surely you desire truth in the inner parts; you teach me wisdom in the inmost place* (Ps. 51:6, NIV).

The Lord desires truth and honesty at the deepest level, and wants us to experience His love, forgiveness, and power in *all* areas of our lives. Experiencing His love does not mean that all of our thoughts, emotions, and behaviors will be pleasant and pure. It means that we can be *real*, feeling pain and joy, love and anger, confidence and confusion.

The Psalms give us tremendous insight about what it means to be honest with the Lord. David and other psalmists wrote and spoke honestly about the full range of their responses to situations. For example, David expressed his anger with the Lord because he felt abandoned by Him:

I say to God my Rock, "Why have you forgotten me?
Why must I go about mourning, oppressed by the enemy?"
Ps. 42:9-10, NIV

At times, David was very angry with others, and expressed that anger to the Lord in terms that reveal the depth of his feelings:

> *Break the teeth in their mouths, O God; tear out, O Lord,*
> *the fangs of the lions!*
> *Let them vanish like water that flows away; when they*
> *draw the bow, let their arrows be blunted.*
> *Like a slug melting away as it moves along, like a stillborn*
> *child, may they not see the sun.*
> *Before your pots can feel the heat of the thorns—whether*
> *they be green or dry—the wicked will be swept away.*
>
> Ps. 58:6-9, NIV

David wrote of his despair about difficult situations:

> *My heart is in anguish within me; the terrors of death*
> *assail me.*
> *Fear and trembling have beset me; horror has*
> *overwhelmed me.*
>
> Ps. 55:4-5, NIV

And he communicated his despair to the Lord:

> *Why do you hide your face and forget our misery and*
> *oppression?*
> *We are brought down to the dust; our bodies cling to the*
> *ground.*
>
> Ps. 44:24-25, NIV

Sometimes, he was confused:

> *How long, O Lord? Will you forget me forever? How*
> *long will you hide your face from me?*

6

How long must I wrestle with my thoughts and every day have sorrow in my heart?

Ps. 13:1-2, NIV

Sometimes, David communicated his love for the Lord:

As the deer pants for streams of water, so my soul pants for you, O God.

My soul thirsts for God, for the living God. When can I go and meet with God?

Ps. 42:1-2, NIV

At times, David trusted in the Lord:

The Lord is my light and my salvation—whom shall I fear? The Lord is the stronghold of my life—of whom shall I be afraid?

When evil men advance against me to devour my flesh, when my enemies and my foes attack me, they will stumble and fall.

Though an army besiege me, my heart will not fear; though war break out against me, even then I will be confident.

Ps. 27:1-3, NIV

At other times, he was filled with praise for God:

I will exalt you, my God the King; I will praise your name for ever and ever.

Every day I will praise you and extol your name for ever and ever.

Great is the Lord and most worthy of praise; his greatness no one can fathom.

Ps. 145:1-3, NIV

These passages demonstrate that God, who spoke of David as a man after His own heart, wants us to be open and honest with Him about *all* of our emotions, not just the pleasant ones.

Some people can read passages like these and begin moving toward healing and health rather quickly. Others, however, may read and study, go to seminars and meetings—they may even be in relationships where they are loved and encouraged—but they may not see substantive change in their lives and patterns of behavior. One reason for this spiritual and emotional inertia is a sense of hopelessness. For various reasons (family background, past experiences, poor modeling), we may have negative presumptions which determine our receptivity to love and truth. In some cases, God's light may have revealed our pain and wall of defenses, but it may not yet have penetrated to our deepest thoughts and beliefs about ourselves. These beliefs may not be clearly articulated, but often reflect misperceptions such as these:

- *God doesn't really care about me.*
- *I am an unlovable, worthless person. Nobody will ever love me.*
- *I'll never be able to change.*
- *I've been a failure all my life. I guess I'll always be a failure.*
- *If people really knew me, they wouldn't like me.*

When the light of love and honesty shines on thoughts of hopelessness, it is often very painful. We begin to admit that we really do feel negatively about ourselves—and have for a long time. But God's love, expressed through His people, and woven into our lives by His Spirit and His Word can, over a period of time, bring healing even to our deepest wounds and instill within us an appropriate sense of self-worth.

The purpose of this book is to provide clear, biblical instruction about the basis of your self-worth by helping you:

1. Identify and understand the nature of man's search for significance.

2.   Recognize and challenge inadequate answers.
3.   Apply God's solutions to *your* search for significance.

This is a process which we will examine throughout the following pages. At this point, simply ask the Lord to give you the courage to be honest. Give Him permission to shine His Spirit's light on your thoughts, feelings, and actions. You may be surprised by additional pain as you realize the extent of your wounds, but our experience of healing can only be as deep as our awareness of the need for it. This takes the power of God's light. Ask Him to turn on the light.

Author's Note:

With the proliferation of books on both secular and Christian psychology, it is helpful to get a perspective of the biblical principles taught in *The Search for Significance*.

Some Christian counselors and authors observe the pain caused by low self-esteem, and try to inflate a person's ego so that he will feel better about himself. Often, this is simply "positive mental attitude" material in Christian lingo.

Some authors and counselors abhor the shallowness of this "let's all feel good about ourselves" approach, but their response takes them to the other extreme. They camp on Christ's teaching that we should hate our lives in order to be His disciples, excluding the abundant and clear teaching of Christ's love, forgiveness, and acceptance. This harsh, out-of-balance approach may be stimulating to someone who is very secure in Christ, but it is devastating to most of us.

A healthy, positive self-esteem is not attained by "feel good" superficiality. On the other hand, a Christ-centered view of ourselves is not detrimental to true discipleship; it is the result of understanding and applying the truths of the Scriptures. A proper view of God and of ourselves enables us to love, obey, and honor Christ with full hearts. Paul wrote, *For through the grace given to me I say to every man among you not to think more highly of himself than he ought to think; but to think so as to have sound judgment* . . . (Rom. 12:3). This sound judgment is not based on either pop psychology or spiritual masochism. Sound judgment is based squarely on God's truth. *The Search for Significance* is designed to present His truth clearly.

Two
Our Search for Significance

Relatively few of us experience the blend of contentment and godly intensity that God desires for each person. From life's outset, we find ourselves on the prowl, searching to satisfy some inner, unexplained yearning. Our hunger causes us to search for people who will love us. Our desire for acceptance pressures us to perform for the praise of others. We strive for success, driving our minds and bodies harder and farther, hoping that because of our sweat and sacrifice, others will appreciate us more.

But the man or woman who lives only for the love and attention of others is never satisfied—at least, not for long. Despite our efforts, we will never find lasting, fulfilling peace if we have to continually prove ourselves to others. Our desire to be loved and accepted is a symptom of a deeper need—the need that often governs our behavior and is the primary source of our emotional pain. Often unrecognized, this is our need for self-worth.

The case of Mark and Beth aptly demonstrates this great need. During their final semester at Cornell University, Mark and Beth fell in love. Beth's eyes sparkled, her walk had that certain lightness, and she found it difficult to concentrate on her studies. As she and Mark gazed into each other's eyes, Beth saw the special affection she had always desired. She felt that her need to feel valued and loved would be fulfilled through their relationship. Likewise, Mark was encouraged and motivated by

Beth's acceptance and admiration of him. With her support, Mark thought he could boldly begin a successful career after graduation.

The summer after they graduated from Cornell, Mark and Beth married, believing their love would provide them both with a permanent sense of self-worth. Unfortunately, they were depending on each other to fill a void that could only be filled by their Creator. Each expected the other to always be loving, accepting, and forgiving, but soon both were disillusioned and even felt betrayed by the other. As the years passed, affirmation was replaced by sarcasm and ridicule. Because each had anticipated that the other would consistently provide love and acceptance, each failure to do so was another brick in their wall of hurt and separation. Recently, Mark and Beth celebrated their tenth wedding anniversary. Sadly, although they had shared ten years with each other, they had experienced very little true, unconditional love for each other. Their search for self-worth and significance ended in despair.

Another example illustrates how the promise of fulfillment through success is an empty one, often resulting in tragic consequences for ourselves and those around us:

Brad and Lisa had been married for twelve years. Brad was a successful lawyer, and Lisa was a homemaker extensively involved in church activities. Their two sons, six-year-old Kyle and eight-year-old David, were well-behaved boys. Although their family appeared to be a model of perfection to those around them, Brad and Lisa were beginning to experience some real problems. True, Brad's law practice was flourishing, but at the expense of Lisa and the boys. He arrived home later and later each evening, and often spent the weekend locked in his office. Brad was driven to succeed, believing that satisfaction and contentment were always just one more trial victory away. But each success gave him only temporary fulfillment. *Maybe the next one....*

Brad would not allow anything to interfere with his success, not even the needs of his family. At first, Lisa seemed to understand. She knew Brad's work was important and hated to protest when he was so busy. Not wanting to burden him, she began to feel guilty for talking to him about

12

family problems. But as the weeks turned into months, and Brad remained obsessed with his work, Lisa became resentful. Even though it was painful, she could overlook her own needs, but the boys needed their father. The family never had time to be together any more, and Brad's promises had begun to sound hollow. "When this big case is over, the pressure will be off," he'd say, but there was always another case. Brad was continually solving other people's problems, but never those of his own family. Realizing that she and the boys weren't important to him, Lisa became bitter and depressed.

As Brad and Lisa's problems persisted, they became obvious to others. Friends began asking Lisa what was wrong. Finding it difficult at first to be honest about the situation, Lisa eventually shared her feelings. She was both hurt and surprised by the glib responses she received from well-meaning but insensitive friends. "Just trust the Lord," one said. Another close friend advised, "You shouldn't have any problems, Lisa. You're a Christian. With God's help, you can work it out."

Like falling on a jagged rock, these comments hurt deeply. Lisa began to doubt herself and wonder if she were capable of building a successful marriage and family. Feeling like a failure, she reasoned that perhaps she deserved a broken marriage; perhaps her problems with Brad were her fault and God was punishing her for her sins.

Confused and frustrated, both Brad and Lisa were searching for significance in their own ways—Brad in his success as an attorney, and Lisa in her success as a wife and mother. Their lives began to reflect that strange combination of hopelessness and compulsion. Sadly, neither Brad nor Lisa realized that their search should both begin and end with God's Word.

In the Scriptures, God supplies the essentials for discovering our true significance and worth. The first two chapters of Genesis recount man's creation, revealing man's intended purpose (to honor God) and man's value (that he is a special creation of God). John 10:10 also reminds us of how much God treasures His creation, in that Christ came so that man might experience "abundant life." However, as Christians, we need to realize that this abundant life is lived in a real world filled with pain, rejection, and failure. Therefore, experiencing the abundant life God intends for us does not mean that our lives will be problem-free. On the contrary, life itself is a series of problems that often act as obstacles to our search for significance, and the abundant life is the experience of God's love, forgiveness, and power in the midst of these problems. The Scriptures warn us that we live within a warfare that can destroy our faith, lower our self-esteem, and lead us into depression. In his letter to the Ephesians, Paul instructs us to put on the armor of God so that we can be equipped for spiritual battle. However, it often seems that unsuspecting believers are the last to know this battle is occurring, and that Christ has ultimately won the war. They are surprised and confused by difficulties, thinking that the Christian life is a playground, not a battlefield.

As Christians, our fulfillment in this life depends not on our skills to avoid life's problems, but on our ability to apply God's specific solutions to those problems. An accurate understanding of God's truth is the first step toward discovering our significance and worth. Unfortunately, many of us have been exposed to inadequate teaching from both religious and secular sources concerning our self-worth. As a result, we may have a distorted self-perception, and may be experiencing hopelessness rather than the rich and meaningful life God intends for us.

Christian psychologist, Lawrence J. Crabb, Jr., describes our need for self-esteem this way: "The basic personal need of each person is to regard himself as a worthwhile human being." And, according to William Glasser, "Everyone aspires to have a happy, successful, pleasurable belief in himself."

Some secular psychologists focus on self-worth with a goal of simply feeling good about ourselves. A biblical self-concept, however, goes far beyond that limited perspective. It is an accurate perception of ourselves, God, and others based on the truths of God's Word. An accurate, biblical self-concept contains both strength and humility, both sorrow over sin and joy about forgiveness, a deep sense of our need for God's grace and a deep sense of the reality of God's grace.

Whether labeled "self-esteem" or "self-worth," the feeling of significance is crucial to man's emotional, spiritual, and social stability, and is the driving element within the human spirit. Understanding this single need opens the door to understanding our actions and attitudes.

What a waste to attempt to change behavior without truly understanding the driving needs that cause such behavior! Yet, millions of people spend a lifetime searching for love, acceptance, and success without understanding the need that compels them. We must understand that this hunger for self-worth is God-given and can only be satisfied by Him. Our value is not dependent on our ability to earn the fickle acceptance of people, but rather, its true source is the love and acceptance of God. He created us. He alone knows how to fulfill *all* of our needs.

In order to fully understand the provisions that God has made for our self-worth, we must look back to man's beginning—to the first man and woman, and their search for significance.

Three

The Origin of the Search

The Old Testament depicts the original incident of sin and the Fall of Man:

> *When the woman saw that the tree was good for food, and that it was a delight to the eyes, and that the tree was desirable to make one wise, she took from its fruit and ate; and she gave also to her husband with her, and he ate.*
> *Then the eyes of both of them were opened, and they knew that they were naked; and they sewed fig leaves together and made themselves loin coverings.*
>
> Gen. 3:6-7

To understand the devastating effects of this event properly, we need to examine the nature of man before sin caused him to lose his security and significance.

The first created man lived in unclouded, intimate fellowship with God. He was secure and free. In all of God's creation, no creature compared to him. Indeed, Adam was a magnificent creation, complete and perfect in the image of God, designed to reign over all the earth (Gen. 1:26-28). Adam's purpose was to reflect the glory of God. Through man, God wanted to demonstrate His holiness (Ps. 99:3-5); love and patience (1 Cor. 13:4); forbearance (1 Cor. 13:7); wisdom (James 3:13, 17); comfort (2 Cor. 1:3-4); forgiveness (Heb. 10:17); faithfulness (Ps. 89:1, 2, 5, 8); and grace (Ps. 111:4). Through his intellect, free will, and emotions, man was to be the showcase for God's glorious character.

Adam was, therefore, a very important creation to God. To meet his needs for companionship and understanding, God created a woman for Adam and gave her to him as his wife. In keeping with their perfect character, God placed Adam and Eve in a perfect environment—a lush, beautiful garden where the Creator Himself provided for their physical needs. Adam and Eve had the challenge and responsibility of supervising this paradise of vegetation and animal life. To satisfy Adam and Eve's spiritual needs, God visited them and talked with them personally. Adam and Eve were perfect in body, mind, and spirit.

Like Adam and Eve, Satan also was created in perfection. At the time of his creation, his name was Lucifer, which means "morning star." He was an angel of the highest rank, created to glorify God. He was clothed with beauty and power, and was allowed to serve in the presence of God. Sadly, Lucifer's pride caused him to rebel against God, and he was cast from heaven with a third of the angels (Is. 14:12-15). When he appeared to Adam and Eve in the garden, it was in the form of a serpent, *more crafty than any beast of the field which the Lord God had made* (Gen. 3:1).

Adam had been given authority over the earth, but if he, like Lucifer, rebelled against God, he would lose both his authority and perfection. He would become a slave to Satan and to sin (Rom. 6:17), and a child of God's wrath (Eph. 2:3). Therefore, destroying man was Satan's way to reign on earth and, he apparently thought, to thwart God's glorious plan for man.

To accomplish his goal, Satan began by deceiving Eve, who fell to the temptation. Eve ate of the tree of the knowledge of good and evil, believing it would make her wise and like God. Adam, however, was not deceived. He deliberately chose to forsake the love and security of God and follow Eve in sin. Paul explained this fact to Timothy:

And it was not Adam who was deceived, but the woman being quite deceived, fell into transgression.

1 Tim. 2:14

In doing this, Adam not only lost the glory God had intended for mankind, but he also forfeited his close communion and fellowship with God. Adam's deliberate rebellion also aided Satan's purpose, giving him power and authority on earth. From that moment on, all history led to a single hill outside of Jerusalem, where God appointed a Savior to pay the penalty for man's sin of rebellion.

Though we justly deserve the wrath of God because of that deliberate rebellion (our attempts to find security and purpose apart from Him), His Son became our substitute, experienced the wrath our rebellion deserves, and paid the penalty for our sins. Christ's death is the most overwhelming evidence of God's love for us. Because Christ paid for our sins, our relationship with God has been restored, and we are able to partake of His nature and character, to commune with Him, and to reflect His love to all the world.

Spread the good news! Man is not lost forever! God has not given up on us! He has bought us out of slavery to sin by the payment of Christ's death on the cross. Satan's rule can be broken and we can reign with Christ. We can be restored to the security and significance for which we have been created—not simply in eternity, but here and now as well.

We must never forget that God wants His children to bear His image and to rule with Him. Adam's sin has had tragic consequences, but through God's plan of redemption, we can still have the unspeakable privilege of relating to Him. God has provided the solution, but the question is this: Will we accept Christ's death as the payment for our sins and discover the powerful implications of our salvation, or will we continue to follow Satan's lies and deceptions?

Perhaps you are unsure of your relationship with God and need to deal conclusively with this choice now. We cannot pay for our sins; Christ has already done this for us as a free gift. Paul wrote to the Ephesian Christians:

> *For by grace* (unmerited favor) *you have been saved*
> (rescued from spiritual death—hell) *through faith* (trust); *and*
> *that not of yourselves, it is the gift of God;*
> *not as a result of works, that no one should boast.*
>
> Eph. 2:8-9

Are you trusting in your own abilities to earn acceptance with God, or are you trusting in the death of Christ to pay for your sins, and the resurrection of Christ to give you new life? Take a moment to reflect on this question: On a scale of 0-100 percent, how sure are you that you would spend eternity with God if you died today? An answer of less than 100 percent may indicate that you are trusting, at least in part, in yourself. You may be thinking, *Isn't it arrogant to say that I am 100 percent sure?* Indeed, it would be arrogance if you were trusting in yourself—your abilities, your actions, and good deeds—to earn your salvation. However, if you are no longer trusting in your own efforts, but in the all-sufficient payment of Christ, then 100 percent certainty is a response of humility and thankfulness, not arrogance.

Reflect on a second question: If you were to die today and stand before God, and He were to ask you, "Why should I let you into heaven?" what would you tell Him? Would you mention your abilities, church attendance, kindness to others, Christian service, abstinence from a particular sin, or some other good deed? Paul wrote to Titus:

> *But when the kindness of God our Savior and His love for*
> *mankind appeared,*
> *He saved us, not on the basis of deeds which we have done*
> *in righteousness, but according to His mercy. . . .*
>
> Titus 3:4-5

We must give up our own efforts to achieve righteousness, and instead believe that Christ's death and resurrection alone are sufficient to pay for our sin and separation from God.

Perhaps you have intellectually believed that Jesus Christ lived 2,000 years ago, performed miracles, died on the cross, and was raised from the dead. Perhaps you have even felt close to God at times in your life. But biblical faith is more than intellectual assent or warm emotions.

Consider the analogy of a wedding: An engaged couple may intellectually know they want to marry each other, and probably feel very close to one another, but until they willfully say, "I do" to each other, they are not married. Many people are at this point in their relationship with Christ. They need to say, *I do* to Him.

If there is any question about whether you have conclusively accepted Christ's substitutionary death to pay for the wrath you deserve for your sins, take some time to think about the two questions we have examined, and reflect on His love and forgiveness. Then, respond by trusting in Christ and accepting His payment for your sins. You can use this prayer to express your faith:

Lord Jesus, I need You. I want You to be my Savior and Lord. I accept Your death on the cross as the complete payment for my sins. Thank You for forgiving me and for giving me new life. Help me to grow in my understanding of Your love and power so that my life will bring honor to You. Amen.

The moment you trust Christ, many wonderful things happen to you:

All your sins are forgiven: past, present, and future (Col. 2:13-14).
You become a child of God (John 1:12; Rom. 8:15).
You receive eternal life (John 5:24).
You are delivered from Satan's domain and transferred into the kingdom of Christ (Col. 1:13).

Christ comes to dwell within you (Col. 1:27; Rev. 3:20).

You become a new creation (2 Cor. 5:17).

You are declared righteous by God (2 Cor. 5:21).

You enter into a love relationship with God (1 John 4:9-11).

You are accepted by God (Col. 1:19-22).

Think on the implications of these truths in your life. Then, thank God for His wonderful grace and experience *the love of Christ which surpasses knowledge* (Eph. 3:19).

Some people may ask, "How does baptism relate to this conversion experience?" Water baptism is a visible demonstration of a believer's internal conversion to Christ. It enables the believer to identify himself with Christ in his culture. The act of baptism symbolizes his being dead, buried, and raised with Christ. In the early church and in some countries today, this identification is a dramatic statement of being severed from the world and being bonded to the body of Christ. In our society, it is still an important step of obedience as we identify ourselves publicly with Christ and His people. (For a sample of passages on Spirit baptism and water baptism, see Acts 8:26-39; Rom. 6:1-4, and 1 Cor. 12:13.)

Four
The Saving Solution vs. Satan's Snare

Satan, the father of lies, twists and distorts the truth so that his deceptions appear to be more reasonable and attractive than the truth. Notice how Satan snared Eve. He told her:

> *For God knows that in the day you eat from it your eyes will be opened, and you will be like God, knowing good and evil.*

Gen. 3:5

Here, Satan directly questioned God's truthfulness, implying that Eve could have greater significance apart from God, and that eating the forbidden fruit would reveal hidden knowledge, enabling her to know good from evil like God Himself.

Being deceived, Eve traded God's truth for the serpent's lie. She ate the forbidden fruit. Then, Adam followed her in sinful rebellion against God, and he, too, ate the forbidden fruit. One of the tragic implications of this event is that man lost his secure status with God and began to struggle with feelings of arrogance, inadequacy, and despair, valuing the opinions of others more than the truth of God. This has robbed man of his true self-worth and has put him on a continual, but fruitless, search for significance through his success and the approval of others.

In one form or another, Satan's lie still thrives today. For example, humanism, the central philosophy of our schools and society, teaches that man is above all else, that he alone is the center of meaning. Teaching that man has meaning totally apart from God, humanism leaves morality, justice, and behavior to the discretion of "enlightened" man and encourages people to worship man and nature rather than God. Living without God's divine truth, humanity sinks lower and lower in depravity, blindly following a philosophy that intends to heighten the dignity of man, but which instead lowers him to the level of animals. Rather than a spiritual and emotional being, man has been classified as merely natural phenomena of time plus chance, no greater than rocks, animals, or clouds. The Apostle Paul described this foolish and demeaning perspective of man in Rom. 1:20-25:

> *For since the creation of the world His invisible attributes, His eternal power and divine nature, have been clearly seen, being understood through what has been made, so that they are without excuse.*
>
> *For even though they knew God, they did not honor Him as God, or give thanks; but they became futile in their speculations, and their foolish heart was darkened.*
>
> *Professing to be wise, they became fools,*
>
> *and exchanged the glory of the incorruptible God for an image in the form of corruptible man and of birds and four-footed animals and crawling creatures.*
>
> *Therefore God gave them over in the lusts of their hearts to impurity, that their bodies might be dishonored among them.*
>
> *For they exchanged the truth of God for a lie, and worshiped and served the creature rather than the Creator, who is blessed forever. Amen.*

In the beginning, God declared that man was created to reign with Him; however, man rejected God's truth and chose instead to believe Satan's lie. Today, man continues to reject God's truth and offer of salvation through Jesus Christ. He chooses instead to trust in his success and the opinions of others to give him a sense of self-worth, though the Scriptures clearly teach that apart from Christ, man is enslaved to sin and condemned to an eternity in hell.

Since the Fall, man has often failed to turn to God for the truth about himself. Instead, he has looked to others to meet his inescapable need for self-worth. *I am what others say I am,* he has reasoned. *I will find my value in their opinions of me.*

Isn't it amazing that we turn to others who have a perspective as limited and darkened as our own to discover our worth! Rather than relying on God's steady, uplifting reassurance of who we are, we depend on others who base our worth on our ability to meet their standards.

Because our performance and ability to please others so dominates our search for significance, we have difficulty recognizing the distinction between our real identity and the way we behave, a realization crucial to understanding our true worth. Our true value is not based on our behavior or the approval of others, but on what God's Word says is true of us.

Our behavior is often a reflection of our beliefs about who we are. It is usually consistent with what we think to be true about ourselves (Prov. 23:7). If we base our worth solidly on the truths of God's Word, then our behavior will often reflect His love, grace, and power. But if we base our worth on our abilities or the fickle approval of others, then our behavior will reflect the insecurity, fear, and anger that comes from such instability.

Though we usually behave in ways that are consistent with our beliefs, at times, our actions may contradict them. For example, we may believe that we are generous and gracious, when we are actually very selfish. Sometimes, our behavior changes what we believe about ourselves. If, for instance, we succeed in a task at which we initially believed we would fail, our confidence may begin to grow and expand to other areas of our lives. Our feelings, behavior, and beliefs all interact to shape our lives.

Our home environment plays a central role in forming our beliefs and emotions, and these can have a powerful impact on our outlook and behavior.

This truth is evident in the case of Scott. Scott grew up in a home without praise, discouraged by his parents whenever he attempted anything new and challenging. After twenty years of hearing, "You'll never be able to do anything, Scott, so don't even try," he believed it himself. Neither Scott nor his parents could later understand why he had flunked out of college and was continually shuffling from one job to another, never able to achieve success. Believing he was doing the best he could do, but suspecting he would always fail, Scott consistently performed according to his self-perception.

Separated from God and His Word, people have only their abilities and the opinions of others on which to base their worth, and the circumstances around them ultimately control the way they feel about themselves.

Take the case of Stacy, a young girl who became pregnant when she was seventeen. Stacy gave her baby up for adoption, and only her family and a few close friends knew of the incident. Several years later, Stacy fell in love with a compassionate man named Ron and married him. Fearing his reaction, she didn't tell Ron about the baby.

Over the years, Stacy concealed her guilt and grief until the pressure finally became so overwhelming that she admitted the entire episode to him.

Surprisingly, Ron did not respond in anger. He understood the agony his wife had carried for so many years and loved her in spite of her past. It was Stacy who could not cope at this point. Unable to accept Ron's forgiveness, and knowing she had failed according to society's standards, Stacy felt unworthy of his love. Stacy refused to forgive herself and chose to leave her husband.

In this case, Stacy fell victim to one of Satan's most effective lies: *Those who fail are unworthy of love and deserve to be blamed and condemned.* Because she failed in her own eyes, Stacy's perception of herself was detrimentally affected.

Each of us has probably failed badly at some point in our lives. Perhaps some particular sin or weakness has caused us to feel condemned and unworthy of love. Without the hope and healing that God can provide, our evaluation of ourselves will eventually lead to despair.

In spite of Adam and Eve's sin, God's plan is to bring man back to the destiny for which he was originally created—to bear His image. To accomplish this, God gives a new nature to all who believe in Christ. This new nature is able to reflect God's character and rule His creation. In Luke 10:19, Jesus spoke of the authority of this new nature when He said, *Behold, I have given you authority to tread upon serpents and scorpions, and over all the power of the enemy, and nothing shall injure you.*

Satan, however, continues to deceive people, including many Christians, into believing that the basis of their worth is their performance and their ability to please others. The equation below reflects Satan's lie:

SELF-WORTH = PERFORMANCE + OTHERS' OPINIONS

Can we overcome Satan's deception and reject this basis of our self-worth? Can we trust God's complete acceptance of us as His sons and daughters, and allow Him to free us from our dependency on success and the approval of others? Rejecting Satan's lie and accepting God's evaluation of us leads to a renewed hope, joy, and purpose in life.

We all have compelling, God-given needs for love, acceptance, and purpose, and most of us will go to virtually any lengths to meet those needs. Many of us have become masters at "playing the game" to be successful and win the approval of others. Some of us, however, have failed and have experienced the pain of disapproval so often that we have given up and have withdrawn into a shell of hurt, numbness, or depression. In both cases, we are living by the deception that our worth is based on our performance and others' opinions—some of us are simply more adept at playing this game than others.

Our attempts to meet our needs for success and approval fall into two broad categories: compulsiveness and withdrawal.

Some people expend extra effort, work extra hours, and try to say just the right thing to achieve success and please those around them. These people may have a compelling desire to be in control of every situation. They are perfectionists. If a job isn't done perfectly, if they aren't dressed just right, if they aren't considered "the best" by their peers, then they work harder until they achieve that coveted status. And woe to the poor soul who gets in their way! Whoever doesn't contribute to their success and acclaim is a threat to their self-esteem—an unacceptable threat. They may be very personable and have a lot of "friends," but the goal of these relationships may not be to give encouragement and love; it may be to manipulate others to contribute to their success. That may sound harsh, but people who are driven to succeed will often use practically everything and everybody to meet that need.

The other broad category is withdrawal. Those who manifest this behavior usually try to avoid failure and disapproval by avoiding risks. They won't volunteer for the jobs that offer much risk of failure. They gravitate toward people who are comforting and kind, skirting relationships that might demand vulnerability, and consequently, the risk of rejection. They may appear to be easygoing, but inside they are usually running from every potential situation or relationship that might not succeed.

Obviously, these are two broad categories. Most of us exhibit some combination of the two behaviors, willing to take risks and work hard in the areas where we feel sure of success, but avoiding the people and situations that may bring rejection and failure.

Rob and Kathy had dated for three years. Kathy was a perfectionist. Her clothes, her hair, her work, her car...and her boyfriend had to be perfect. Rob, a good-natured, fun-loving fellow, was not as concerned with such details. Predictably, the more intense Kathy became about having everything and everybody "just right," the more passive and easygoing Rob became. This spiral of intensity and passivity continued until Rob and Kathy hit rock bottom.

After several weeks of counseling, Kathy saw that her perfectionism came from a misplaced base of security: her performance instead of Christ. But Rob said that he didn't have a problem with performance. He certainly didn't have a compelling drive to succeed, and he didn't pressure people around him to "get their act together." In the midst of these explanations, I asked, "But Rob, what about your tendency to withdraw? Why do you think you do that?" It still didn't compute.

Finally, after several months, Rob understood. He based his security on his performance just as much as Kathy did, but he handled it differently. She became more compulsive to have things "just right," while he withdrew to avoid failure. Both slowly began to recognize the root of their problems, and through months of encouragement and honest interaction, they started believing that their worth is secure in Christ. Today, Kathy is less intense about her performance, and Rob doesn't run from failure as much as he used to. They are learning to channel their intensity toward the right things: Christ and His kingdom.

When we base our security on success and others' opinions, we become dependent on our abilities to perform and please others. We develop a *have-to* mentality: *I have to do well on this exam (or my security as a "good student" will be threatened); I have to make that deal (or it will mean that my boss will think I am a failure); My father (or mother, spouse, or friend) has to appreciate me and be happy with my decisions (because I cannot cope with his disapproval).*

Our self-esteem and view of God are usually a mirror of our parents' attitudes toward us. Those who are loved and affirmed by their parents tend to have a fairly healthy self-concept, and usually find it easy to believe that God is loving and powerful. Those whose parents have been neglectful, manipulative, or condemning usually seem to feel that they have to earn a sense of worth, and that God is aloof, demanding, and/or cruel.

Our parents are our models of the character of God. When we do not have that fundamental sense of feeling lovable and protected by them, then we tend to base our self-worth on how well we perform and please others, instead of on what the sovereign God of the universe, our all-wise, omniscient Savior says of us.

We do not *have to* be successful or *have to* be pleasing to others to have a healthy sense of self-esteem and worth. That worth has freely and conclusively been given to us by God. Failure and/or the disapproval of others can't take it away! Therefore, we can conclude, *It would be nice to be approved by my parents* (or whomever), *but if they don't approve of me, I'm still loved and accepted by God.* Do you see the difference? The *have-to* mentality is sheer slavery to performance and the opinions of others, but we are secure and free in Christ. We don't *have to* have success or anyone else's approval. Of course, it would be nice to have success and approval, but the point is clear: Christ is the source of our security; Christ is the basis of our worth; Christ is the only One who promises and never fails.

The transition from the slavery and compulsion of a *have-to* mentality to the freedom and strength of a *want-to* motivation is a process. Bondage to such thinking is often deeply rooted in our personalities, patterns of behavior, and ways of relating to other people. These patterns of thinking, feeling, and responding—learned over time—flow as naturally as the course of rainwater in a dry desert riverbed. Changing them requires time, the encouragement of others, the truth and application of God's Word, and the power of God's Spirit.

This book is dedicated to the process of understanding, applying, and experiencing the foundational truths of God's Word. In the remaining chapters, we will examine the process of hope and healing. We will also identify four specific false beliefs generated by Satan's deception. In addition, we will discover God's gracious, effective, and permanent solution to our search for significance.

Five
The Process of Hope and Healing

In the first chapter of this book, we saw that Tim Woodall had a car accident late in the evening on a lonely country highway in East Texas. Tim was broken and bleeding, but because he was in shock, he was completely unaware of the extent of his injuries.

Aided by their car's headlights, the Johnsons realized that Tim needed immediate attention, and took him to the nearest hospital. Tim stayed there for three days. The doctors waited for the swelling in his leg to go down before putting it in a cast, and then kept him for observation, knowing that the blow to his head might have caused a concussion.

Tim's wife took him home from the hospital, and after a week or so, the pain in his leg began to subside, and the stitches were removed from his head and arm. Tim wasn't sure which was worse: limping around on his crutches, or looking at himself in the mirror. The nurse had shaved a portion of his scalp for the stitches, and his new appearance took some getting used to for everyone—but especially for Tim.

Three months later, Tim's cast was removed, and a new hairstyle gave him a far more presentable appearance. It was several more months before he was able to build strength back into his leg muscles again, but after awhile, the only marks left from the accident were the scars, which weren't readily noticeable.

Tim's rehabilitation was a process. It wasn't spontaneous. His injuries required attention and expert care. Emotional, spiritual, and relational healing is a process, too. It doesn't happen overnight, but it can happen.

Several elements are required for emotional healing. These are not consecutive steps to be accomplished one after the other. They are ingredients which promote healing by working together simultaneously over a period of time. These elements are honesty; affirming relationships; right thinking; the Holy Spirit's power, strength, and wisdom; and time. If any of these is missing, then the healing process will be hindered, if not completely stifled.

Let's examine these ingredients:

Honesty

As we noted in chapter 1, we can apply and experience healing only to the depth that we are aware of our need for it. If we are completely unaware of our need, we won't seek a solution. If we are only superficially aware of our need and honest about it, we may only seek (and find) superficial remedies. But if we are encouraged to be honest about our painful needs at a deeper level, then we can experience the power of healing and comfort at that level.

Affirming Relationships

People seldom have the objectivity and the courage to be honest about reality in their lives without some affirmation from others. The love, strength, and honesty we find in other people are tangible expressions of those traits that are characteristic of God. A friend, a small group, a pastor, or a counselor who won't be frustrated by our slow progress—and who won't give us quick and easy solutions—is a valuable find! (Of course, it is always wise to use discretion and discernment regarding what and with whom we share. The act of sharing is a responsibility.) Pray that God will provide a person or group of persons with whom you can be open and honest, who can objectively listen to you and share with you, and who will encourage you to make real, rather than superficial progress.

Right Thinking

Many of us are unaware of what we really believe about God and about ourselves. We often say what we don't mean, and mean what we don't say. God's Word is our guide. It is truly *a lamp for our feet and a light for our path* (Ps. 119:105). And yet, we often experience difficulty in applying scriptural concepts to our lives because of the elaborate array of defenses we have structured over the years to protect ourselves. It is important to understand that Scripture can be used to identify and attack these defensive barriers, enabling us to experience an open and honest relationship with God:

> *For the word of God is living and active and sharper than any two-edged sword, and piercing as far as the division of soul and spirit, of both joints and marrow, and able to judge the thoughts and intentions of the heart.*
>
> *And there is no creature hidden from His sight, but all things are open and laid bare to the eyes of Him with whom we have to do.*
>
> Heb. 4:12-13

The Holy Spirit

Deep, spiritual healing requires giving attention to the whole man, to his emotional, relational, physical, and spiritual needs. The Holy Spirit is given by God to communicate His love, light, forgiveness, and power to our deepest needs. This spiritual aspect of healing is perhaps the most fundamental, because our view of God (and subsequent relationship with Him) can determine the quality and degree of health we experience in every other area of our lives.

Some of us believe that the Holy Spirit's ministry is characterized only by positive, pleasant emotions like love and joy. However, one of the miracles of the Holy Spirit's work is that of producing honesty and courage in our lives as we grapple with the reality of pain. He is the Spirit of truth, not denial, and He enables us to experience each element of the healing process as He gives us wisdom, strength, and encouragement through God's Word and other people.

Time

If we were computers, solutions to our problems would be produced in microseconds. People, however, don't change that quickly. The agrarian metaphors given in the Scriptures depict *seasons* of planting, weeding, watering, growth, and harvesting. Farmers don't expect to plant seeds in the morning and harvest their crops that afternoon. Seeds must go through a complete cycle of growth, receiving plenty of attention in the process, before they mature. In this age of instant coffee, microwave dinners, and instant banking, we tend to assume that spiritual, emotional, and relational health will be instantaneous. These unrealistic expectations only cause discouragement and disappointment.

Although this book's primary focus is on the cognitive, or right-thinking, aspect of our spiritual growth, we need to remember that all of these elements are required to produce growth and health. Our growth will be stunted and superficial if we don't give proper emphasis to honesty about our emotions, affirming relationships, right thinking promoted through biblical study and application, the ministry of the Holy Spirit, and time.

Some of us seem to respond to this environment of growth very quickly; others, after a few weeks or months; and still others, never at all. Why the difference? Why are some of us able to apply principles of growth so much more readily that others?

Again, differing factors will produce a variety of responses from different people. Those who respond quickly may not be as wounded as others, or they may already be in an environment which has prepared them for relatively rapid growth.

Some of us are in situations where one or more elements of growth are in some way missing or lacking. We may be trying to deal with our difficulties alone. We may be depending on a rigid structure of discipline for positive change, instead of blending a healthy combination of our responsibility with the Holy Spirit's enabling power. We may be expecting too much too soon, and may be experiencing disappointment with our slow results. Some of us may, in fact, be ready to quit the growth process entirely.

Those of us who can't seem to get the light turned on have the greatest difficulty in beginning this process. We can't see our problems. We may recognize that something is wrong, but can't pinpoint exactly what. Or, our defense mechanisms of denial may be so strong that we're unable to see any needs in our lives at all.

A young man asked me, "What about people from very stable backgrounds? They don't wrestle with the difficulties you're talking about, do they?"

"All of us have a fallen, sinful nature," I responded. "Because of that, we all wrestle to some degree with the fears of failure and rejection, and with feelings of inadequacy, guilt, and shame. Those from stable, loving families are usually better able to determine what their difficulties are, and be honest about them, than those who are shackled by the defense mechanisms that are often developed in dysfunctional families.

"Those from abusive, manipulative, or neglectful families have far more to overcome than those from a healthier home environment," I explained. "Alcoholism, divorce, sexual abuse, physical abuse, workaholism, drug abuse, and other major family disorders leave deep wounds. Many people from backgrounds like these have suppressed their intense hurt and anger for so long that they are simply out of touch with the reality in their lives. Therefore, just as a broken arm requires more time, attention, and therapy for healing than does a small abrasion, people suffering from deep emotional, spiritual, and relational injuries need more time, attention, love, and encouragement than those with more minor wounds. Though the process for recovery may take longer, enjoying health in these areas is still possible if all the elements of healing are applied over its duration."

Another person asked, "Why doesn't just understanding these issues work? Why isn't knowledge enough to produce change?"

"Man is a relational, physical, emotional, and spiritual being," I said. "We develop and learn and grow best in an environment of honesty, love, and affirmation, where all aspects of our nature are given the encouragement to heal."

A woman asked me, "What do I need to do to begin seeing some results?"

"Put yourself in an environment of growth, which includes all the elements of honesty, affirming relationships, right thinking, the ministry of the Holy Spirit, and time. I can't tell you how or when growth will come—but I know that it will come if you are patient and persistent."

A businessman asked, "Why do I not see much change in my life?"

After talking with him for awhile, three issues surfaced which can be common to many of us: First, this gentleman had advanced significantly in his profession by performing well and pleasing people. Although he had received promotions, raises, prestige, and comfort, he still wasn't happy. Yet, it was difficult for him to consider living by a pattern of behavior other than that which had seemingly brought him so far.

In addition, this man was afraid of how he might respond to the generosity of God's love and freedom. He feared that he would either abuse God's grace or be so changed by it that some of his friends and business associates might make fun of him and ultimately reject him.

Finally, he feared that if he did respond wholeheartedly to God's love, the Lord might test his faith by making his life miserable. "I couldn't stand that," he told me. "My life is painful now, but at least I'm used to it. If I surrender completely to God, my life might get totally out of control."

These and many other reasons make the process of spiritual, relational, emotional, and mental health elusive to many people. But again, honesty is our starting point. When we are willing to be open about our thoughts and fears, we generally find that others have thought and felt much the same way.

Our growth toward wholeness and maturity is a journey which won't be completed until we join the Lord in heaven. The Apostle Paul understood this, and saw himself as being in the middle of this process. He wrote to the Philippian believers:

> *Not that I have already obtained it, or have already become perfect, but I press on in order that I may lay hold of that for which I was laid hold of by Christ Jesus.*
>
> Phil. 3:12

If Paul, the foremost missionary and writer of much of the New Testament, saw himself as being "in the process," we can be encouraged to continue in the process toward change as well. It will help to have reasonable expectations about our progress. Sometimes, we will experience flashes of insight and spurts of growth, but the process of healing and renewal will more often be slow and methodical. Our emotions, too, may occasionally be very pleasant and positive, but when God's light shines on another area of hurt in our lives, we will likely experience another round of pain and anger. Remember that healing can only continue as we put ourselves in an environment characterized by honesty, affirming relationships, right thinking, the Holy Spirit's love and power, and time.

Introduction to Chapters Six, Seven, Eight, and Nine

It is often helpful to see a general outline when attempting to grasp new concepts. In the next four chapters, we will examine four false beliefs resulting from Satan's deceptions with some of the consequences that accompany these beliefs. Finally, we will examine God's specific solution for our false belief system, and apply this through some practical exercises.

Remember that the specific consequences of false beliefs and resulting actions vary from person to person, depending on family background, personality traits, other relationships, and many other factors. Likewise, the application of biblical truths will vary according to the perception of the individual, the degree of his or her emotional, spiritual, and relational health, and the process by which the cognitive, relational, spiritual, and emotional elements are incorporated into his or her life. All of this takes time, but health and hope are worth it!

The chart on the following pages provides an overview of the next four chapters:

Chapter	False Beliefs
Six The Performance Trap	*I must meet certain standards in order to feel good about myself.*
Seven Approval Addict	*I must be approved (accepted) by certain others to feel good about myself.*
Eight The Blame Game	*Those who fail are unworthy of love and deserve to be punished.*
Nine Shame	*I am what I am. I cannot change. I am hopeless.*

Consequences	God's Answer
The fear of failure; perfectionism; driven to succeed; manipulating others to achieve success; withdrawal from risks.	Justification *Justification means that God has not only forgiven me of my sins, but has also granted me the righteousness of Christ. Because of justification, I bear Christ's righteousness and am, therefore, fully pleasing to the Father* (Rom. 5:1).
The fear of rejection; attempting to please others at any cost; overly sensitive to criticism; withdrawing from others to avoid disapproval.	Reconcilation *Reconciliation means that although I was at one time hostile toward God and alienated from Him, I am now forgiven and have been brought into an intimate relationship with Him. Consequently, I am totally accepted by God* (Col. 1:21-22).
The fear of punishment; punishing others; blaming others for personal failure; withdrawal from God and others; driven to avoid failure.	Propitiation *Propitiation means that Christ satisfied God's wrath by His death on the cross; therefore, I am deeply loved by God* (1 John 4:9-11).
Feelings of shame, hopelessness, inferiority; passivity; loss of creativity; isolation; withdrawal from others.	Regeneration *Regeneration means that I am a new creation in Christ* (John 3:3-6).

One man asked me, "Why do you include only *four* false beliefs? Doesn't Satan also use many others?"

"Yes," I replied, "he uses an endless variety of deceptions to confuse and distort the truth of God; yet, in my study of the Scriptures and through my interaction with people, these four seem to represent the central issues we struggle with in our desire for significance."

"Can a person experience more than one false belief in a given situation?" he asked.

"Yes, of course," I said. "Many of life's circumstances reveal that we are basing our response to a situation on more than one of Satan's lies. Usually, however, close examination will reveal that one may be more foundational. For example, I may be afraid to fail, but the real reason I fear failure could be that I'm afraid that my failure might result in the disapproval of others."

We will explore the interrelationship of misconceptions after we've identified the false beliefs in the following chapters.

Six

The Performance Trap

Most of us are unaware of how thoroughly Satan has deceived us. He has led us blindly down a path of destruction, captives of our inability to meet our standards consistently, and slaves of low self-esteem. Satan has shackled us in chains that keep us from experiencing the love, freedom, and purposes of Christ.

In Col. 2:8, Paul warns:

> *See to it that no one takes you captive through philosophy and empty deception, according to the tradition of men, according to the elementary principles of the world, rather than according to Christ.*

Indeed, we've reached a true mark of maturity when we begin testing the deceitful thoughts of our minds against the Word of God. We no longer have to live by our fleshly thoughts; we have the mind of Christ (1 Cor. 2:16). Through His Spirit, we can challenge the indoctrinations and traditions that have long held us in guilt and condemnation. We can then replace those deceptions with the powerful truths of the Scriptures.

A primary deception all of us tend to believe is that success will bring fulfillment and happiness. Again and again, we've tried to measure up, thinking that if we could meet certain standards, we would feel good about ourselves. But again and again, we've failed and have felt miserable. Even if we succeed on a fairly regular basis, occasional failure may be so devastating that it dominates our perception of ourselves.

Consciously or unconsciously, all of us have experienced this feeling that we must meet certain arbitrary standards to attain self-worth. Failure to do so threatens our security and significance. Such a threat, real or perceived, results in a fear of failure. At that point, we are accepting the false belief: *I must meet certain standards in order to feel good about myself.* When we believe this about ourselves, Satan's distortion of truth is often reflected in our attitudes and behavior.

Because of our unique personalities, we each react very differently to this deception. As we saw in a previous chapter, some of us respond by becoming slaves to perfectionism—driving ourselves incessantly toward attaining goals.

Perfectionists can be quite vulnerable to serious mood disorders, and often anticipate rejection when they believe they haven't met the standards they are trying so hard to attain. Therefore, perfectionists tend to react defensively to criticism and demand to be in control of most situations they encounter. Because they are usually more competent than most, perfectionists see nothing wrong with their compulsions. "I just like to see things done well," they claim. There is certainly nothing inherently wrong with doing things well; the problem is that perfectionists usually base their self-worth on their ability to accomplish a goal. Therefore, failure is a threat and is totally unacceptable to them.

Karen, a wife, mother, and civic leader, seemed ideal to everyone who knew her. She was a perfectionist. Her house looked perfect, her kids were spotless, and her skills as president of the Ladies' Auxiliary were superb. In each area of her life, Karen was always in charge, always successful. However, one step out of the pattern she had set could lead to a tremendous uproar. When others failed to comply with her every demand, her condemnation was quick and cruel.

One day, her husband decided that he couldn't stand any more of Karen's hypercritical behavior. He wanted an understanding wife to talk and share with, not an egocentric, self-driven perfectionist. Friends later could not understand why he chose to leave his seemingly perfect wife.

Like Karen, many high achievers are driven beyond healthy limitations. Rarely able to relax and enjoy life, they let their families and relationships suffer as they strive to accomplish often unrealistic goals.

On the other hand, the same false belief *(I must meet certain standards to feel good about myself)* that drives many to perfectionism sends others into a tailspin of despair. They rarely expect to achieve anything or to feel good about themselves. Because of their past failures, they are quick to interpret present failures as an accurate reflection of their worthlessness. Fearing more failure, they often become despondent and stop trying.

Finally, the pressure of having to meet self-imposed standards in order to feel good about ourselves can result in a rules-dominated life. Individuals caught in this trap often have a set of rules for most of life's situations, and continually focus their attention on their performance and ability to adhere to their schedule. Brent, for example, made a daily list of what he could accomplish if everything went perfectly. He was always a little tense because he wanted to use every moment effectively to reach his goals. If things didn't go well, or if someone took too much of his time, Brent got angry. Efficient, effective use of time was his way of attaining fulfillment, but he was miserable. He was constantly driven to do more, but his best was never enough to satisfy him.

Brent believed that accomplishing goals and making efficient use of his time were what the Lord wanted him to do. Due to stress, he occasionally thought that *something* wasn't quite right, but his solution was to try harder, make even better use of his time, and be even more regimented in his adherence to self-imposed rules.

Brent's focus was misdirected. The focus of the Christian life should be on Christ, not on self-imposed regulations. Our experience of Christ's lordship is dependent on our moment-by-moment attention to His instruction, not our own regimented schedule.

As these cases demonstrate, the false belief, *I must meet certain standards in order to feel good about myself*, results in a fear of failure. How affected are you by this belief? Take the following test to determine how strongly you fear failure.

FEAR OF FAILURE TEST

Read each of the following statements; then, from the top of the test, choose the term which best describes your response. Put the number above that term in the blank beside each statement.

1	2	3	4	5	6	7
Always	Very Often	Often	Sometimes	Seldom	Very Seldom	Never

_____ 1. Because of fear, I often avoid participating in certain activities.

_____ 2. When I sense that I might experience failure in some important area, I become nervous and anxious.

_____ 3. I worry.

_____ 4. I have unexplained anxiety.

_____ 5. I am a perfectionist.

_____ 6. I am compelled to justify my mistakes.

_____ 7. There are certain areas in which I feel I *must* succeed.

_____ 8. I become depressed when I fail.

_____ 9. I become angry with people who interfere with my attempts to succeed, and as a result, make me appear incompetent.

_____ 10. I am self-critical.

_____ Total (Add up the numbers you have placed in the blanks.

Interpretation of Score
    If your score is...

57-70

    God has apparently given you a very strong appreciation for His love and unconditional acceptance. You seem to be freed from the fear of failure that plagues most people. (Some people who score this high are either greatly deceived, or have become callous to their emotions as a way to suppress pain.)

47-56

    The fear of failure controls your responses rarely, or only in certain situations. Again, the only major exceptions are those who are not honest with themselves.

37-46

    When you experience emotional problems, they may relate to a sense of failure or to some form of criticism. Upon reflection, you will probably relate many of your previous decisions to this fear. Many of your future decisions will also be affected by the fear of failure unless you take direct action to overcome it.

27-36

    The fear of failure forms a general backdrop to your life. There are probably few days that you are not affected in some way by this fear. Unfortunately, this robs you of the joy and peace your salvation is meant to bring.

0-26

    Experiences of failure dominate your memory, and have probably resulted in a great deal of depression. These problems will remain until some definitive action is taken. In other words, this condition will not simply disappear; time alone cannot heal your pain. You need to experience deep healing in your self-concept, in your relationship with God, and in your relationships with others.

EFFECTS OF THE FEAR OF FAILURE

The fear of failure can affect our lives in many ways. The following list is not an exhaustive discussion of its resulting problems, nor are these problems explained completely by the fear of failure. However, recognizing and confronting the fear of failure in each of these experiences could result in dramatic changes.

Perfectionism

Again, one of the most common symptoms of the fear of failure is perfectionism, an unwillingness to fail. This tendency suffocates joy and creativity. Because any failure is perceived as a threat to our self-esteem, we develop a propensity to focus our attention on the one area in which we failed rather than those in which we did well. Areas where we often tend to be perfectionistic include work, punctuality, house-cleaning, our appearance, hobbies and skills—practically anything and everything!

Perfectionists often appear to be highly motivated, but their motivations usually come from a desperate attempt to avoid the low self-esteem they experience when they fail.

Avoiding Risks

Another very common result of the fear of failure is a willingness to be involved in only those activities that can be done well. New, challenging activities are avoided because the risk of failure is too great. Avoiding risks may seem comfortable, but it severely limits the scope of our creativity, self-expression, and service to God.

Anger, Resentment

When we fail, when others contribute to our failure, or when we are injured or insulted in some way, anger is a normal response. Feeling angry

48

isn't wrong. In fact, the Apostle Paul encouraged the Ephesians to *be angry*, but quickly followed that encouragement with the admonition to avoid expressing anger in a sinful, or hurtful, way (Eph. 4:26).

Unfortunately, rather than using our anger constructively, many of us either vent our fury without a thought of its result, or we suppress it. Repressed anger eventually leads to retaliatory outbursts, deep and seething resentment, and/or depression.

Anxiety and Fear

Failure is often the source of self-condemnation and the disapproval of others, both of which are severe blows to a self-worth based on personal success and approval. If failure is great enough or occurs often enough, it can harden into a negative self-concept in which we will expect to fail at virtually every endeavor. This negative self-concept perpetuates itself and leads to a downward spiral of anxiety about our performance and fear of disapproval from others.

Pride

When we base our self-worth on our performance and are successful, we often develop an inflated view of ourselves: pride. Some of us may persist in this self-exaltation through any and all circumstances; for most of us, however, this sense of self-esteem lasts only until our next failure (or risk of failure). The self-confidence that most of us try to portray is only a facade to hide our fear of failure and insecurity.

Depression

Depression is generally a result of anger turned inward and/or a deep sense of loss. Experiencing failure and fearing subsequent failure can lead to deep depression. Once depressed, many become emotionally numb and passive in their actions, believing there is no hope for change. Occasionally, depressed people may also exhibit outbursts of anger resulting from failure. Generally, depression is the body's way of blocking psychological pain by numbing physical and emotional functions.

Low Motivation

Much of what is known as low motivation or laziness is better understood as hopelessness. If people believe they will fail, they have no reason to exert any effort. The pain they endure for their passivity seems relatively minor and acceptable compared to the agony of genuinely trying and failing.

Sexual Dysfunction

The emotional trauma caused by failure can cause disturbances in sexual activity. Then, rather than experience the pain of failing sexually, many tend to avoid sex altogether.

Chemical Dependency

Many people attempt to ease their pain and fear of failure by using drugs or alcohol. Those who abuse alcohol often do so with the false notion that it will increase their level of performance, thus enhancing their attempts at being successful. Alcohol, however, is a depressant, and actually decreases the user's performance ability.

Stimulants also are often used to increase productivity. Users of these drugs are likely to consume larger doses on an increasingly regular basis until they are addicted. This is because natural physiological processes deplete bodily resources during drug binges, so that when users come down from the chemical's "high" effect, they crash and are unable to rise to any occasion without it.

Taking a drink—like playing tennis, jogging, seeing a movie, or reading a book—can be a refreshing means of temporary escape. The problem is that chemical substances are addictive, and often, easily abused. For those who find themselves trapped by chemical dependency, what may have begun as a pleasurable means of temporary escape, or an effort to remove pressures to perform, ends with the despair of realizing an inability to cope without the substance. This pain-pleasure cycle continues, slowly draining the life from its victim.

Because of their euphoric effect, alcohol or drugs may give us an illusion that we are "on top of the world." But success, or the idea of success, regardless of how it is achieved, cannot dictate our sense of self-esteem.

In the case of chemical substances, cocaine users provide a clear example of this truth. A major reason for cocaine's popularity is its ability to produce feelings of greater self-esteem. However, it is interesting to note that a number of highly successful people use this drug. If success truly provided a greater sense of self-esteem, these people would probably not be in the market for the drug in the first place.

As long as we operate according to Satan's lies, we are susceptible to the fear of failure. Our personal experience of this fear is determined by the difference between our performance standards and our ability to meet those standards.

Although we all will continue to experience the fear of failure to some degree, we must realize that as Christians, we have the power provided by the Holy Spirit to lay aside deceptive ways of thinking, and be renewed in our minds by the truth of God's Word (Rom. 12:2; Eph. 4:21-25). For our benefit, God often allows us to experience circumstances which will enable us to recognize our blind adherence to Satan's deceptions. Many times, these circumstances seem very negative, but through them, we can learn valuable, life-changing truths. In Ps. 107:33-36, we see a poetic example of this:

> *He changes rivers into a wilderness, and springs of water into a thirsty ground;*
> *A fruitful land into a salt waste, because of the wickedness of those who dwell in it.*
> *He changes a wilderness into a pool of water, and a dry land into springs of water;*
> *And there He makes the hungry to dwell, so that they may establish an inhabited city.*

Has your fruitful land become a salt waste? Maybe God is trying to get your attention to teach you a tremendously important lesson: that success or failure is not the basis of your self-worth. Maybe the only way you can learn this lesson is by experiencing the pain of failure. In His great love, God leads us through experiences that are difficult but essential to our growth and development.

The more sensitive you become to the fear of failure and the problems it may cause, the more you will understand your own behavior as well as that of others.

GOD'S ANSWER: JUSTIFICATION

If we base our self-worth on our ability to meet standards, we will try to compensate, either by avoiding risks, or by trying to succeed no matter what the cost. Either way, failure looms as a constant enemy.

As I reflect on my life, I recall being especially fearful of failure during my teenage years. This fear was apparent in many areas of my life, but particularly in athletics.

Because I was, from an early age, taller than most children, many perceived that I would be a basketball player. I practiced a lot during that time, and became a very skilled player. In the process, I learned that I could do many things on the court in practice, or while playing with friends, that I would never even attempt to try during a game, when the pressure was intense. I was afraid of failure, and that fear prevented me from doing many things in basketball which I had the ability to do.

The same fear, I now realize, has prevented me from attempting achievement in several other areas of my life. Although God has enabled me to conquer this fear on many occasions, there are still times when I struggle with the risk of failing. This may be surprising to some who have known me and have thought of me as being successful. Yet, those who have experienced great success know that making an important achievement is often followed by the fear of losing that attainment.

Success truly does not reduce the amount of fear we experience in our lives. In fact, success often causes our fears to escalate because we perceive that we have more to lose.

Thankfully, God has a solution for the fear of failure! He has given us a secure self-worth totally apart from our ability to perform. We have been *justified*, placed in right standing before God through Christ's death on the cross, which paid for our sins. But God didn't stop with our forgiveness; He also granted us the very righteousness of Christ (2 Cor. 5:21)!

Visualize two ledgers: on one is a list of all your sins; on the other, the righteousness of Christ. Now exchange your ledger for Christ's. This exemplifies justification—transferring our sin to Christ and His righteousness to us. In 2 Cor. 5:21, Paul wrote:

> *He made Him* (Christ) *who knew no sin to be sin on our behalf, that we might become the righteousness of God in Him.*

I once heard a radio preacher berate his congregation for their hidden sins. He exclaimed, "Don't you know that someday you're going to die and God is going to flash all your sins upon a giant screen in heaven for all the world to see?" How tragically this minister misunderstood God's gracious gift of justification!

Justification carries no guilt with it, and has no memory of past transgressions. Christ paid for all of our sins at the cross—past, present, and future. Hebrews 10:17 says, *And their sins and their lawless deeds I will remember no more.* We are completely forgiven by God!

As marvelous as it is, justification means more than forgiveness of sins. In the same act of love through which God forgave our sin, He also provided for our *righteousness*: the worthiness to stand in God's presence.

By imputing righteousness to us, God attributes Christ's worth to us. The moment we accept Christ, God no longer sees us as condemned sinners. Instead, we are forgiven, we receive Christ's righteousness, and God sees us as creatures who are fully pleasing to Him.

God intended that Adam and his descendants be righteous people, fully experiencing His love and eternal purposes. But sin short-circuited that relationship. God's perfect payment for sin has since satisfied the righteous wrath of God, enabling us to again have that status of righteousness, and to delight in knowing and honoring the Lord.

God desires for those of us who have been redeemed to experience the realities of His redemption. We are forgiven and righteous because of Christ's sacrifice; therefore, we are pleasing to God in spite of our failures. This reality can replace our fear of failure with peace, hope, and joy. Failure need not be a millstone around our necks. Neither success nor failure is the proper basis of our self-worth. Christ alone is the source of our forgiveness, freedom, joy, and purpose.

God works by *fiat*, meaning that He can create something from nothing by simply declaring it into existence. God spoke and the world was formed. He said, "Let there be light," and light appeared. The earth is no longer void because God sovereignly created its abundance.

In the same way, we were condemned, but now we are declared righteous! Romans 5:1 refers to us as *having been justified by faith*, a statement in the past perfect tense. Therefore, if we have trusted in Christ for our salvation, we each can say with certainty, *I am completely forgiven, and am fully pleasing to God.*

Some people have difficulty thinking of themselves as being pleasing to God because they link *pleasing* so strongly with performance. They tend to be displeased with anything short of perfection in themselves, and suspect that God has the same standard.

The point of justification is that we can never achieve perfection on this earth; even our best efforts at self-righteousness are as filthy rags to God (Is. 64:6). Yet, He loves us so much that He appointed His Son to pay for our sins and give to us His own righteousness, His perfect status before God.

This doesn't mean that our actions are irrelevant, and that we can sin all we want. Our sinful actions, words, and attitudes grieve the Lord, but our status as holy and beloved children remains intact. In His love, He disciplines and encourages us to live godly lives—both for our good and for His honor.

The Apostle Paul was so enamored with his forgiveness and righteousness in Christ that he was intensely motivated to please God by his actions and his deeds. In 1 Cor. 6:19-20; 2 Cor. 5:9; Phil. 3:8-11, and in other passages, Paul strongly stated his desire to please, honor, and glorify the One who had made him righteous.

Some people may read these statements and become uneasy, believing that I am discounting the gravity of sin. As you will see, I am not minimizing the destructive nature of sin, but am simply trying to elevate our view of the results of Christ's payment on the cross. Understanding our complete forgiveness and acceptance before God does not promote a casual attitude toward sin. On the contrary, it gives us a greater desire to live for and serve the One who died to free us from sin. Let's look at some strong reasons to obey and serve God with joy:

REASONS FOR OBEDIENCE

The love of God and His acceptance of us is based on grace, His unmerited favor. It is not based on our ability to impress God through our good deeds. But if we are accepted on the basis of His grace and not our deeds, why *should* we obey God? Here are six compelling reasons to obey Him:

Christ's Love

Understanding God's grace compels us to action because love motivates us to please the One who has so freely loved us. When we experience love, we usually respond by seeking to express our love in return. Our obedience to God is an expression of our love for Him (John 14:15, 21), which comes from an understanding of what Christ has accomplished for us on the cross (2 Cor. 5:14-15). We love because He first loved us and clearly demonstrated His love for us at the cross (1 John 4:16-19). Understanding this will highly motivate us to serve Him.

This great motivating factor is missing in many of our lives because we don't really believe that God loves us unconditionally. We expect His love to be conditional, based on our ability to earn it.

Our experience of God's love is based on our perception. If we believe that He is demanding or aloof, we will not be able to receive His love and tenderness. Instead, we will either be afraid of Him or angry with Him. Faulty perceptions of God often prompt us to rebel against Him.

Our image of God is the foundation for all of our motivations. As we grow in our understanding of His unconditional love and acceptance, we will be better able to grasp that His discipline is prompted by care, not cruelty. We will also be increasingly able to perceive the contrast between the joys of living for Christ and the destructive nature of sin. We will be motivated to experience eternal rewards *where neither moth nor rust destroys* (Matt. 6:20). And we will want our lives to bring honor to the One who loves us so much.

Sin Is Destructive

Satan has effectively blinded man to the painful, damaging consequences of sin. The effects of sin are all around us, yet many continue to indulge in the sex, status- and pleasure-seeking, and rampant self-centeredness that cause so much anguish and pain. Satan contradicted God in the Garden when he said, *You surely shall not die!* (Gen. 3:4). Sin is pleasant, but only for a season. Sooner or later, sin will result in some form of destruction.

Sin is destructive in many ways. Emotionally, we may experience the pain of guilt and shame and the fear of failure and punishment. Mentally, we may experience the anguish of flashbacks. We may also expend enormous amounts of time and energy thinking about our sins and rationalizing our guilt. Physically, we may suffer from psychosomatic illnesses or experience pain through physical abuse. Sin may also result in the loss of property, or even the loss of life. Relationally, we can alienate ourselves from others. Spiritually, we grieve the Holy Spirit, lose our testimony, and break our fellowship with God. The painful and destructive effects of sin are so profound that why we don't have an aversion to it is a mystery!

The Father's Discipline

Our loving Father has given us the Holy Spirit to convict us of sin. Conviction is a form of God's discipline, and serves as proof that we have become sons of God (Heb. 12:5-11). It warns us that we are making choices without regard to either God's truth or sin's consequences. If we choose to be unresponsive to the Holy Spirit, our heavenly Father will discipline us in love. Many people do not understand the difference between discipline and punishment. The following chart shows their profound contrasts:

	PUNISHMENT	DISCIPLINE
SOURCE:	God's Wrath	God's Love
PURPOSE:	To Avenge a Wrong	To Correct a Wrong
RELATIONAL RESULT:	Alienation	Reconciliation
PERSONAL RESULT:	Guilt	A Righteous Lifestyle
DIRECTED TOWARD:	Non-Believers	His Children

Jesus bore all the punishment we deserved on the cross; therefore, we no longer need to fear punishment from God for our sins. We should seek to do what is right so that our Father will not have to correct us through discipline, but when we are disciplined, we should remember that God is correcting us in love. This discipline leads us to righteous performance, a reflection of Christ's righteousness in us.

His Commands for Us Are Good

God's commands are given for two good purposes: to protect us from the destructiveness of sin, and to direct us in a life of joy and fruitfulness. We have a wrong perspective if we only view God's commands as restrictions in our lives. Instead, we must realize that His commands are guidelines, given so that we might enjoy life to the fullest.

God's commands should never be considered as a means to gain His approval.

In today's society, we have lost the concept of doing something because it is the right thing to do. Instead, we do things in exchange for some reward or favor, or to avoid punishment. Wouldn't it be novel to do something simply because it is the right thing to do? God's commands are holy, right, and good, and the Holy Spirit gives us the wisdom and strength to keep them. Therefore, since they have value in themselves, we can choose to obey God and follow His commands.

Eternal Rewards

Yet another compelling reason to live for God's glory is the fact that we will be rewarded in heaven for our service to Him. Two passages clearly illustrate this fact:

> *For we must all appear before the judgment seat of Christ, that each one may be recompensed for his deeds in the body, according to what he has done, whether good or bad.*
>
> 2 Cor. 5:10

> *Now if any man builds upon the foundation with gold, silver, precious stones, wood, hay, straw,*
> *each man's work will become evident; for the day will show it, because it is to be revealed with fire; and the fire itself will test the quality of each man's work.*
> *If any man's work which he has built upon it remains, he shall receive a reward.*
> *If any man's work is burned up, he shall suffer loss; but he himself shall be saved, yet so as through fire.*
>
> 1 Cor. 3:12-15

Through Christ's payment for us on the cross, we have escaped eternal judgment; however, our actions will be judged at the judgment seat of Christ. There, our performance will be evaluated, and rewards presented for service to God. Rewards will be given for deeds that reflect a desire to honor Christ, but deeds performed in an attempt to earn God's acceptance, earn the approval of others, or meet our own standards will be rejected by God and consumed by fire.

Christ Is Worthy

Our most noble motivation for serving Christ is simply that He is worthy of our love and obedience. The Apostle John recorded his vision of the Lord and his response to His glory:

> *After these things I looked, and behold, a door standing open in heaven, and the first voice which I had heard, like the sound of a trumpet speaking with me, said, "Come up here, and I will show you what must take place after these things."*
>
> *Immediately I was in the Spirit; and behold, a throne was standing in heaven, and One sitting on the throne.*
>
> *And He who was sitting was like a jasper stone and a sardius in appearance; and there was a rainbow around the throne, like an emerald in appearance.*
>
> *And around the throne were twenty-four thrones; and upon the thrones I saw twenty-four elders sitting, clothed in white garments, and golden crowns on their heads. . . .*
>
> *And when the living creatures give glory and honor and thanks to Him who sits on the throne, to Him who lives forever and ever,*
>
> *the twenty-four elders will fall down before Him who sits on the throne, and will worship Him who lives forever and ever, and will cast their crowns before the throne, saying,*
>
> *"Worthy art Thou, our Lord and our God, to receive glory and honor and power; for Thou didst create all things, and because of Thy will they existed, and were created."*
>
> Rev. 4:1-4, 9-11

59

Christ is worthy of our affection and obedience. There is no other person, no goal, no fame or status, and no material possession that can compare with Him. The more we understand His love and majesty, the more we will praise Him and desire that He be honored at the expense of everything else. Our hearts will reflect the psalmist's perspective:

> *Whom have I in heaven but Thee? And besides Thee, I desire nothing on earth. . . .*
> *But as for me, the nearness of God is my good; I have made the Lord God my refuge, that I may tell of all Thy works.*
> Ps. 73:25, 28

A SUMMARY

We obey God because...

1. Christ's love motivates us to live for Him.
2. Sin is destructive and should be avoided.
3. Our Father lovingly disciplines us for wrongdoing.
4. His commands for us are good.
5. We will receive eternal rewards for obedience.
6. He is worthy of our obedience.

Obeying Christ for these reasons is not a self-improvement program. The Holy Spirit gives us encouragement, wisdom, and strength as we grow in our desire to honor the Lord.

A BEGINNING EXERCISE

How can we begin to experience God's freedom from our fear of failure? How can we begin to live in the light of our justification? Reflecting on the following passage of Scripture will help us to get started:

For as he thinks within himself, so he is.

Prov. 23:7

From this passage of Scripture, and from what we know about ourselves, we can draw the following conclusions and applications:

1. Though some of us are more reflective than others, most of us spend a great deal of time thinking about our performance.

2. We have a choice: We can use the same method we have always used to evaluate ourselves and others (Our Self-Worth = Performance + Others' Opinions), or we can adopt God's evaluation (Our Self-Worth = God's Truth About Us).

3. If we want our lives to be what God has designed them to be, then we must use His truth as our standard of evaluation, rather than our own judgment.

4. To accomplish this change in mindset, we need to apply the following action points:

    a) Memorize this statement: *I have great worth apart from my performance because Christ gave His life for me, and therefore, imparted great value to me. I am deeply loved, fully pleasing, totally forgiven, accepted, and complete in Christ.* Repeat this statement to yourself several times each day for two or three weeks.

    b) Each day, tell those in your family whom you know are Christians, "You are deeply loved, fully pleasing, totally forgiven, accepted, and complete in Christ."

5.   As you do this, these truths can begin to positively reinforce your view of yourself, your relationship with God, and your relationships with others.

6.   Failures, both in your own life and in the lives of your family, can be seen as opportunities to apply this biblical value system. The affirmation of God's love and acceptance can be powerful in shaping a healthy self-concept!

God has given us the Bible as a guidebook. By understanding biblical truths, we will be able to identify the deceptions of Satan; then, we can begin to reject these lies and replace them with the eternal truths of God's Word. This process is not easy, but it is essential to our sense of self-worth and our desire to honor Christ.

Seven
Approval Addict

Our self-concept is determined not only by how we view ourselves, but by how we think others perceive us. Basing our self-worth on what we believe others think of us causes us to become addicted to their approval.

Randy felt like a vending machine. Anyone wanting something could pull an invisible lever and get it. On the job, Randy was always doing other people's work for them. At home, his friends continually called on him to help them with odd jobs. His wife had him working weekends so that she could continue in the lifestyle to which she had grown accustomed. Even people in Randy's church took advantage of him, knowing that they could count on "good old Randy" to head a number of the programs they planned. What was the problem? Was Randy simply a self-sacrificing saint? On the surface, yes; in reality, no. Randy deeply resented those people who, by demanding so much from him, left him little time for himself. Yet, he just couldn't say no. He longed for the approval of others and believed that by agreeing to their every wish, he would win that approval.

Randy typifies many of us. We spend much of our time building relationships, striving to please people and win their respect. And yet, after all of our sincere, conscientious effort, it takes only one unappreciative word from someone to ruin our sense of self-worth. How quickly an insensitive word can destroy the self-assurance we've worked so hard to achieve!

The world we live in is filled with people who demand that we please them in exchange for their approval and acceptance. Such demands often lead us directly to a second false belief: *I must be approved by certain others to feel good about myself.*

We are snared by this lie in many subtle ways. Believing it causes us to bow to peer pressure in an effort to gain approval. We may join clubs and organizations, hoping to find a place of acceptance for ourselves. We often identify ourselves with social groups, believing that being with others like ourselves will assure our acceptance and their approval.

Many people have admitted that their experimentation with drugs or sex is a reaction to their need to belong. However, drugs and sexual promiscuity promise something they can't fulfill, and experimentation only leaves these people with pain, and usually, a deeper need for self-worth and acceptance.

Another symptom of our fear of rejection is our inability to give and receive love. We find it difficult to open up and reveal our inner thoughts and motives because we believe that others will reject us if they know what we are really like. Therefore, our fear of rejection leads us to superficial relationships or isolation. The more we experience isolation, the more we need acceptance. Psychologist Eric Fromm once wrote, "The deep need of man is the need to overcome separateness, to leave the prison of his aloneness."

The fear of rejection is rampant, and loneliness is one of the most dangerous and widespread problems in America today. Some estimate that loneliness has already reached epidemic proportions, and say that if it continues to spread, it could seriously erode the emotional strength of our country. Loneliness is not relegated only to unbelievers. Ninety-two percent of the Christians attending a recent Bible conference admitted in a survey that feelings of loneliness were a major problem in their lives. All shared a basic symptom: a sense of despair at feeling unloved and a fear of being unwanted or unaccepted. This is a tragic commentary on the people about whom Christ said:

> *By this all men will know that you are my disciples, if you*
> *have love for one another.*
>
> John 13:35

For the most part, our modern society has responded inadequately to rejection and loneliness. Our response has been outer-directed, meaning that we try to copy the customs, dress, ideas, and behavioral patterns of a particular group, allowing the consensus of the group to determine what is correct for us. But conforming to a group will not fully provide the security we are so desperately seeking. Only God can provide that through His people, His Word, His Spirit, and His timing. Turning to others for what only God can provide is a direct result of our acceptance of Satan's lie:

Self-Worth = Performance + Others' Opinions

Living according to the false belief, *I must be approved by certain others to feel good about myself,* causes us to fear rejection, conforming virtually all of our attitudes and actions to the expectations of others. How are you affected by this belief? Take the test on the following page to determine how strongly you fear rejection.

FEAR OF REJECTION TEST

Read each of the statements below; then, from the top of the test, choose the term which best describes your response. Put the number above that term in the blank beside each statement.

1	2	3	4	5	6	7
Always	Very Often	Often	Sometimes	Seldom	Very Seldom	Never

_____ 1. I avoid certain people.

_____ 2. When I sense that someone might reject me, I become nervous and anxious.

_____ 3. I am uncomfortable around those who are different from me.

_____ 4. It bothers me when someone is unfriendly to me.

_____ 5. I am basically shy and unsocial.

_____ 6. I am critical of others.

_____ 7. I find myself trying to impress others.

_____ 8. I become depressed when someone criticizes me.

_____ 9. I always try to determine what people think of me.

_____ 10. I don't understand people and what motivates them.

_____ Total (Add up the numbers you have placed in the blanks.

Interpretation of Score
If your score is...

57-70

God has apparently given you a very strong appreciation for His love and unconditional acceptance. You seem to be freed from the fear of rejection that plagues most people. (Some people who score this high are either greatly deceived, or have become callous to their emotions as a way to suppress pain.)

47-56

The fear of rejection controls your responses rarely, or only in certain situations. Again, the only major exceptions are those who are not honest with themselves.

37-46

When you experience emotional problems, they may relate to a sense of rejection. Upon reflection, you will probably relate many of your previous decisions to this fear. Many of your future decisions will also be affected by the fear of rejection unless you take direct action to overcome it.

27-36

The fear of rejection forms a general backdrop to your life. There are probably few days that you are not in some way affected by this fear. Unfortunately, this robs you of the joy and peace your salvation is meant to bring.

0-26

Experiences of rejection dominate your memory and have probably resulted in a great deal of depression. These problems will persist until some definitive action is taken. In other words, this condition will not simply disappear; time alone cannot heal your pain. You need to experience deep healing in your self-concept, in your relationship with God, and in your relationships with others.

EFFECTS OF THE FEAR OF REJECTION

Virtually all of us fear rejection. We can fall prey to it even when we've learned to harden our defenses in anticipation of someone's disapproval. Neither being defensive nor trying to please another person's every whim is the answer to this problem. These are only coping mechanisms which prevent us from dealing with the root of our fear.

Rejection is a type of communication. It conveys a message that someone else is unsatisfactory to us; that he or she doesn't measure up to a standard we've created or adopted. Sometimes, rejection is willfully used as an act of manipulation designed to control someone else. Usually, rejection is manifested by an outburst of anger, a disgusted look, an impatient answer, or a social snub. Whatever the form of behavior, it communicates disrespect, low value, and lack of appreciation. Nothing hurts quite like the message of rejection.

If this is true, why do we reject others so frequently? Again, rejection can be a very effective, though destructive, motivator. Without raising a finger, we can send the message that our targeted individual doesn't meet our standards. We can harness this person's instinctive desire for acceptance until we have changed and adapted his or her behavior to suit our tastes and purposes. This is how rejection enables us to control the actions of another human being.

Many misguided preachers have used rejection and guilt as a forceful means of motivation. They expound upon our weaknesses, our failures, our unworthiness, and our inability to measure up to Christ's high standards. Not only is our performance declared unworthy, but we are left feeling denounced, devalued, and devastated. As a result, thousands who have been broken by this rejection have left the Church without understanding Christ's accepting, unconditional love—a love that never uses condemnation to correct behavior.

However, rejection and guilt are only effective motivators as long as people are near us. This is why certain parental techniques of guilt motivation produce results only until the child matures and gains more freedom. With freedom, he is able to remove himself physically from his parents. Unrestrained, he then can do as he pleases.

In this instance, both the parents and the child need to experience God's love and forgiveness. His grace and power can give understanding and strength, so that they can forgive each other, forgive themselves, and exhibit strong, loving relationships.

Another damaging result of rejection is isolation. Michael, for example, was raised in a broken home and had lived with his father since he was six years old. It wasn't that Michael's father wanted him, but his mother was too busy to care for him. Shortly after the divorce, Michael's father married another woman with three children. She began to resent spending any time or effort on Michael. She favored her own children at his expense.

It was no surprise, then, that when Michael grew up and married a beautiful girl who truly loved him, he was cautious about sharing his love with her. Michael had experienced the pain of rejection all of his life and now, because he feared rejection, he withheld his love from someone he truly cared for. Michael was afraid of becoming too close to his wife, because if she rejected him, the pain would be too much for him to bear.

How do you react to the fear of rejection? Some of us project a cool, impervious exterior, and consequently, never develop deep, satisfying relationships. Some of us are so fearful of rejection that we withdraw and decline almost everything, while others continually say yes to everyone, hoping to gain their approval. Some of us are shy and easily manipulated; some of us are sensitive to criticism and react defensively. A deep fear of rejection may prompt hostility and promote the development of nervous disorders.

Our fear of rejection will control us to the degree by which we base our self-worth on the opinions of others rather than on our relationship with God. Our dependence on others for value brings bondage, while abiding in the truths of Christ's love and acceptance brings freedom and joy.

In Gal. 1:10, Paul clearly draws the line concerning our search for approval:

> *For am I now seeking the favor of men, or of God? Or am*
> *I striving to please men? If I were still trying to please men, I*
> *would not be a bond-servant of Christ.*

According to this passage, we can ultimately seek either the approval of men or the approval of God as the basis of our self-worth. We cannot seek both. God wants to be the Lord of our lives, and He is unwilling to share that rightful lordship with anyone else. Therefore, the only way we can overcome the fear of rejection is to value the constant approval of God over the conditional approval of people.

My desire for the approval of others has often been so great that I sometimes joke about having been born an "approval addict." Growing up, I had the feeling that I didn't fit in; that I was "different" from others; that there was, therefore, something inherently wrong with me. I felt inadequate and tried to win the approval of others, desperately hoping that this would compensate for the negative feelings I had about myself.

But ironically, the conditional approval of others was never enough to satisfy me. Instead, being praised only reminded me of the disapproval I might encounter if I failed to maintain what I had achieved. I was thus compelled to work even harder at being successful. I occasionally find myself falling into this pattern of behavior even now, despite my improved knowledge, experience, and relationship with God.

Many people may be surprised to learn this, perhaps assuming that reading this book and completing its exercises will forever liberate them from the propensity to base their self-worth on the approval of others.

I don't believe that any of us will gain complete freedom from this tendency until we see the Lord. Our God-given instinct to survive compels us to avoid pain. Knowing that rejection and disapproval bring pain, we will continue our attempts to win the esteem of others whenever possible. The good news is that because we are fully pleasing to God—a fact we will examine later in this chapter—we need not be devastated when others respond to us in a negative way.

As we grow in our relationship with God, the Holy Spirit will continue teaching us how to apply this liberating truth to different aspects of our lives at an increasingly deeper level. In fact, one evidence of His work within us is the ability to see new areas of our lives in which we are allowing the opinions of others to determine our sense of worth. With spiritual maturity, we will more often be able to identify these areas and choose to find our significance in God's unconditional love for us and complete acceptance of us. However, profound changes in our value system take honesty, objectivity, and prolonged, persistent application of God's Word.

Before we examine God's solution to our fear of failure, we must first identify and understand how this fear is manifested in our lives. Similar to the fear of failure, the fear of rejection can affect us in many ways. The explanations of the following symptoms are not exhaustive, but are intended to demonstrate how rejection can trigger certain problems in our lives:

Anger, Resentment, Hostility

Anger is usually our most common response to rejection. Some of us are not honest about our anger. We may deny its existence, suppress it, and assume that it will go away. We may vent our anger in destructive explosions of wrath. Or, we may use sarcasm or neglect to express anger in a more subtle way. If we don't resolve our anger through honesty and forgiveness, we can become deeply hostile and resentful. One motive for retaining anger is the desire for revenge.

Being Easily Manipulated

Those who believe that their self-worth is based on the approval of others are likely to do virtually anything to please people. They truly believe they will be well-liked if they agree to every request of those who are, consciously or not, manipulating them. Many of these people often despise those who are being manipulative, and resent what they feel they have to do to earn their approval.

Codependency

In families affected by dependency on alcohol, drugs, work, or any other compulsion, family members often develop behavioral patterns to rescue the dependent person from the consequences of his or her behavior. This compulsive rescuing, called *codependency*, effectually allows the dependent person to continue acting destructively, and keeps him or her in need of being habitually rescued, so that the pattern continues.

Avoiding People

Among the most common ways people react to their fear of rejection is to avoid others, thereby avoiding the risk of rejection. Some people avoid others overtly, spending most of their time alone, but most people try to lower the risk of rejection by having superficial relationships. They may be around people much of the time, and they may be considered socially adept because they know how to make friends easily, but their friends are never really able to know them because they hide behind a wall of words, smiles, and activities. These people are usually quite lonely in the midst of all their "friends."

Control

In an effort to avoid being hurt, many people constantly try to maintain control of others and dominate most situations. They have become adept in exercising control by dispensing approval or disapproval, unwilling to let others be themselves and make their own decisions without their consent. Because such people are actually very insecure, lack of control is an unacceptable threat to them.

Depression

Depression is the result of a deep sense of loss or repressed, pent-up anger. When anger is not handled properly, the body and mind respond to its intense pressure, and the person's emotions and sense of purpose become dulled.

The reason we experience the fear of rejection and its accompanying problems is because we believe Satan's lie that our *Self-Worth = Performance + Others' Opinions.* We crave love, fellowship, and intimacy, and turn to others to meet those needs. However, the problem with basing our worth on the approval of others is that God is the only One who loves and appreciates us unconditionally. He has provided a solution to the fear of rejection.

GOD'S ANSWER: RECONCILIATION

God's solution to the fear of rejection is based on Christ's sacrificial payment for our sins. Through this payment, we find forgiveness, reconciliation, and total acceptance through Christ. *Reconciliation* means that those who were enemies have become friends. Paul described our transformation from enmity to friendship with God:

> *And although you were formerly alienated and hostile in mind, engaged in evil deeds,*
> *yet He has now reconciled you in His fleshly body through death, in order to present you before Him holy and blameless and beyond reproach.*
>
> Col. 1:21-22

As I talked with Pam, it became obvious that she did not understand this great truth of reconciliation. Three years after she married, Pam had committed adultery with a coworker. Although she had confessed her sin to God and to her husband, and had been forgiven, guilt continued to plague her, making it difficult for her to feel acceptable to God. Four years after the affair, she still could not forgive herself for what she had done.

Sitting in my office, we explored her reluctance to accept God's forgiveness.

"It sounds as though you believe that God can't forgive the sin you committed," I said.

"That's right," she replied. "I don't think He ever will."

"But God doesn't base His love and acceptance of us on our performance," I said. "If any sin is so filthy and vile that it makes us less acceptable to Him, then the cross is insufficient. If the cross isn't sufficient for all sin, then the Bible is in error when it says that He forgave *all* your sins (Col. 2:13-15). God took our sins and cancelled them by nailing them to Christ's cross. In this way, God also took away Satan's power to condemn us for sin. So you see, nothing you will ever do can nullify your reconciliation and make you unacceptable to God."

Our unconditional acceptance in Christ is a profound, life-changing truth. Salvation is not simply a ticket to heaven. It is the beginning of a dynamic new relationship with God. *Justification* is the doctrine that explains the judicial facts of our forgiveness and righteousness in Christ. *Reconciliation* explains the relational aspect of our salvation. The moment we receive Christ by faith, we enter into a personal relationship with Him. We are united with God in an eternal and inseparable bond (Rom. 8:38-39). We are bound in an indissoluble union with Him, as fellow heirs with Christ. The Holy Spirit has sealed us in that relationship, and we are absolutely secure in Christ. Ephesians 1:13-14 states:

> ...*Having also believed, you were sealed in Him with the Holy Spirit of promise,*
>
> *who is given as a pledge of our inheritance, with a view to the redemption of God's own possession, to the praise of His glory.*

Recently, in a group prayer meeting, someone prayed, "Thank you, God, for accepting me when I am so unacceptable." This person understood that we cannot earn God's acceptance by our own merit, but seemed to have forgotten that we are unconditionally accepted in Christ. We are no longer unacceptable—the point of the cross. Through Christ's death and resurrection, we have become acceptable to God. This did not occur because God decided He could overlook our sin, but because Christ forgave all of our sins so that He could present us to the Father, holy and blameless.

There is no greater theme in Scripture than the reconciliation of man to God. Open your Bible and read for yourself. The following passages are taken from the New American Standard Version of Scripture. Study them, and then answer the question after each one:

Ps. 103:12—What happens to our transgressions?_____
_____

Matt. 26:28—Why was Christ's blood shed?_____
_____

John 3:16—What is God's promise?_____
_____

John 5:24—What is the promise to the person who knows and believes?_____
_____

John 10:27-29—What do His sheep have? Will they perish?_____
_____

Acts 10:43—Of what did the prophets bear witness?_____
_____

Acts 13:39—What does belief do?_____
_____

Rom. 3:23, 24—By what are we justified?_____
_____

Rom. 4:7—Who is blessed?_____
_____

Rom. 5:10—Through what are we reconciled?_____
_____

Rom. 8:15-17—Describe the nature of our relationship with God:____
_____

Rom. 8:33—Who shall accuse us?_____
_____

Rom. 8:38-39—Of what is Paul convinced?_____
_____

2 Cor. 5:17,19,21—Describe what we are in Christ:_____
_____

Gal. 2:16—On what basis are we justified?_____
_____

Gal. 2:16—What part do works play in justification?_____
_____

Gal. 3:6—On what basis did Abraham receive righteousness?_____

_____

Eph. 1:7—According to what do we receive forgiveness?_____

_____

Eph. 2:8-9—On what basis can we boast?_____

_____

Heb. 9:22—What would you have to do in order to receive forgiveness?

_____

Heb. 10:18—After forgiveness, what is to be our offering for sin?_____

_____

Heb. 12:2—Who is the perfecter of our faith?_____

_____

1 Pet. 1:3-4—Of what is Peter convinced?_____

_____

Because of reconciliation, we are completely acceptable to God and are completely accepted by God. As these passages illustrate, we enjoy a full and complete relationship with Him, and in this relationship, His determination of our value is not based on our performance.

However, we may question what this relationship means as we attempt to apply it in our day-to-day experience. Let's analyze this issue:

When we are born again as spiritual beings in right standing with God, we are still tilted toward the world's way of thinking. Because we have been conditioned by the world's perspective and values, we find it hard to break away. Indeed, when Paul wrote the Christians at Corinth, he called them *men of flesh*. Though born of the Spirit, and equipped with all provisions in Christ, these individuals had yet to develop into the complete, mature believers God intended them to be (1 Cor. 3:1-4).

Many of us are like the Christians at Corinth. We still try to obtain our significance the world's way, through success and approval. Often, we look only to other believers rather than to Christ Himself. We learn to use the right Christian words, claim divine power and guidance, and organize programs, and yet so often, our spiritual facade lacks depth and substance. Our spiritual activities become human efforts lacking the real touch of the Master. In effect, we live a lie.

The desire for success and approval constitutes the basis of an addictive, worldly self-worth. Certainly, withdrawal from this dependency may cause us some pain as we change the basis of our self-worth, yet we will begin to discover true freedom and maturity in Christ only when we understand that our lives mean much more than what success or the approval of others can bring.

We can do nothing to contribute to Christ's free gift of salvation; furthermore, if we base our self-worth on the approval of others, then we are actually saying that our ability to please others is of greater value than Christ's payment. We are the sinners, the depraved, the wretched, and the helpless. He is the loving Father, the seeking, searching, patient Savior who has made atonement for the lost, and has extended to us His grace and sonship. We add nothing to our salvation. It is God who seeks us out, convicts us of sin, and reveals Himself to us. It is God who gives us the very faith with which to accept Him. Our faith is simply our response to what He has done for us.

So then, our worth lies in the fact that Christ's blood has paid for our sins; therefore, we are reconciled to God. We are accepted on that basis alone, but does this great truth indicate that we don't need other people in our lives? On the contrary, God very often uses other believers to demonstrate His love and acceptance to us. The strength, comfort, encouragement, and love of Christians toward one another is a visible expression of God's love. However, our acceptance and worth are not *dependent* on others' acceptance of us, even if they are fellow believers! Whether they accept us or not, we are *still* deeply loved, completely forgiven, fully pleasing, totally accepted, and complete in Christ. *He alone* is the final authority on our worth and acceptance.

THE ROLE OF RELATIONSHIPS

For many of us, the unconditional love, forgiveness, and acceptance of Christ seems abstract, and is difficult to comprehend. We may understand the premise of these character traits, but may still be unable to incorporate them into our personal experience. Often, we can trace this difficulty to our parental relationships.

God intends for parents to model His character to their children. According to Scripture, parents are to give their children affection, compassion, protection, provision, and loving discipline. When parents provide this kind of environment in their home, children are usually able to transfer these perceptions to the character of God, and believe that He is loving, compassionate, protective, gracious, and a loving disciplinarian. In turn, they are often able to model these characteristics to their own children.

Many of us, however, have not received this parental model of God's character. On an extremely wide spectrum, some of us have had relatively healthy relationships with our parents, while others have experienced various forms of neglect, condemnation, and manipulation. Still others have suffered the deeper wounds of sexual abuse, physical abuse, or abandonment. The greater the degree of dysfunction (or poor modeling) in a family, the greater the potential for emotional, spiritual, and relational wounds. Put another way, the poorer the parental modeling of God's love, forgiveness, and power, the greater our difficulty in experiencing and applying these characteristics in our lives.

Instead of being refreshed by the truth of God's love, if we have been deeply wounded, we may recoil from it, believing that we are unlovable. We may be fearful of reaching out and being hurt again. Whatever the cause, the result is withdrawal from the very idea of being loved and accepted.

Those who have received poor parental modeling need new models—loving Christian friends—to experience the love and grace of God. Through His body of believers, God often provides us with models of His love, so that our perception of His character can be slowly reshaped into one that is more accurate, resulting in a healthier relationship with Him. Then, our deep emotional, spiritual, and relational wounds can begin to heal, and we can more fully experience God's unconditional love.

Some of us are already involved in strong relationships with people who are understanding and patient with us; some of us haven't yet been able to cultivate relationships like these, and are still looking. If this is your situation, you may need to find a pastor or counselor who can help you get started, possibly by directing you to one or more believers who can minister to you. A small fellowship group or Bible study is often an excellent resource for intimate sharing, comfort, and encouragement. If you have tried to cultivate healthy relationships, but haven't found any yet, don't give up! The Lord wants all of us to be in an environment where we can experience more of His love through our relationships with other believers.

If you ask God for guidance, and are willing to continue putting forth the effort, He will lead you to some people who can provide this kind of an environment for you in His perfect time.

Healthy vs. Unhealthy Relationships

Because many of us are so vulnerable when we begin allowing ourselves to experience the pain that usually accompanies growth, it is wise to have a basic understanding of healthy and unhealthy relationships.

We must first understand that while God often demonstrates His love and affirmation for us through believers and non-believers alike, His desire is that our relationships with others will enable us to know Him more fully. His work through others is, in part, to serve as a channel by which we can better understand His divine love and acceptance of us. Sadly, we are all prone to miss His message and mistake His messenger(s) as the source of our fulfillment. When this misperception is carried to an extreme, we can fall into *emotional dependency*, "the condition resulting when the ongoing presence and/or nurturing of another is believed necessary for personal security."[1]

In his book, *The Four Loves*, C.S. Lewis described the difference between lovers and friends:

Lovers are always talking to one another about their love; Friends hardly ever about their Friendship. Lovers are normally face to face, absorbed in each other; Friends, side by side, absorbed in some common interest. Above all, Eros (while it lasts) is necessary between two only. But two, far from being the necessary number for Friendship, is not even the best.[2]

This well describes the difference between healthy and unhealthy friendship, whether sex comes into the picture or not. Healthy relationships are turned outward, rather than inward. Healthy relationships encourage individuality rather than conformity, and are concerned with independence, rather than emotional dependence. Healthy relationships point one's focus to the Lord and pleasing Him, rather than toward the friendship and pleasing one another.

How do we know when we've crossed the line from a healthy relationship to one that is emotionally dependent? When either party in a relationship:[3]

- experiences frequent jealousy, possessiveness and a desire for exclusivism, viewing other people as a threat to the relationship.
- prefers to spend time alone with this friend and becomes frustrated when this does not happen.
- becomes irrationally angry or depressed when this friend withdraws slightly.
- loses interest in a friendship other than this one.
- experiences romantic or sexual feelings leading to fantasy about this person.
- becomes preoccupied by the person's appearance, personality, problems, and interests.

- is unwilling to make short- or long-range plans that do not include the other person.
- is unable to see the other's faults realistically.
- becomes defensive about this relationship when asked about it.
- displays physical affection beyond what is appropriate for a friendship.
- refers frequently to the other in conversation; feels free to "speak for" the other.
- exhibits an intimacy and familiarity with this friend that causes others to feel uncomfortable or embarrassed in their presence.

Our relationships with one another are very important to God; so much so, that He has placed unity among the brethren as a priority in our relationship with Him (see Matt. 5:23-24). This is because God has reconciled us to Himself as a *body* in Christ (Eph. 2:16), and therefore intends for us to interact as *members of one another* (Eph. 4:25).

Pray that God will guide you to relationships which will encourage you to be honest; practice the truth of His Word; affirm you, and thereby help you develop an appropriate love for yourself; and compel you to focus on Him as the gracious provider of your needs. Eventually, your gratitude will motivate you to practice pleasing Him rather than other people.

A BEGINNING EXERCISE

How do we learn to reject Satan's lie, *I must be approved by certain others to feel good about myself*? How can we begin to practically apply the great truth of our reconciliation to Almighty God? The following exercise will help you begin to experience the freedom and joy of reconciliation.

The thirteenth chapter of First Corinthians describes God's unconditional love and acceptance of us. To personalize this passage, replace the word *love* with *My Father*. Then, memorize the following, and when fear comes to you, recall the love and kindness of God:

My Father is very patient and kind.

My Father is not envious, never boastful.

My Father is not arrogant.

My Father is never rude, nor is He self-seeking.

My Father is not quick to take offense.

My Father keeps no score of wrongs.

My Father does not gloat over my sins, but is always glad when truth prevails.

My Father knows no limit to His endurance, no end to His trust.

My Father is always hopeful and patient.

As you memorize this passage, ask God to show you if your perception of Him is in error in any way. This will enable you to have a more accurate perception of God, and will help you to experience more of His unconditional love and acceptance.

Eight
The Blame Game

Our perception of success and failure is often our primary basis for evaluating ourselves and others. If we believe that performance reflects one's value, and that failure makes one unacceptable and unworthy of love, then we will usually feel completely justified in condemning those who fail, including ourselves. Self-condemnation may include name-calling *(I'm so stupid! I can't do anything right!)*, making self-deprecating jokes or statements, or simply never allowing any room for error in our performance. With others, we may be harsh (physically or verbally abusive), or relatively subtle (sarcastic or silent). But any form of condemnation is a powerfully destructive force which communicates, *I'll make you sorry for what you did.*

Matt made a serious mistake early in his life and was never able to overcome it. At age fourteen, he and several friends from school stepped inside a downtown department store and tried to slip out with some cassette tapes without paying for them. They made it to the glass doors past the cashier's stand before a security guard caught them and escorted all of them into the manager's office.

Matt never heard the end of the incident. Every time he made a mistake at home, his father reminded him of what he had done. "You're a colossal failure!" his father would scream. "You've got no values whatsoever! You're a liar and a thief, and you'll never amount to anything!"

Matt was never able to forget his humiliation. At age twenty, he sat in my office and told me very seriously that on some days, he was happy until he realized that he was feeling good. Believing that he had no right to feel good about himself, he would then begin to feel depressed again.

"After all," he reflected, "no one as worthless as I am should feel good about himself."

Like so many others, Matt had been brainwashed and broken by the false belief: *Those who fail are unworthy of love and deserve to be punished.*

Whether consciously or unconsciously, we all tend to point an accusing finger, assigning blame for virtually every failure. Whenever we fail to receive approval for our performance, we are likely to search for a reason, a culprit, a scapegoat. More often than not, we can find no one but ourselves to blame, so the accusing finger points right back at us. Self-condemnation is a severe form of punishment.

If possible, we will often try to place the blame on others and fulfill the law of retribution—that people should get what they deserve. For most of our lives, we have been conditioned to make someone pay for failures or shortcomings. When a deadline is missed at work, we let everyone know it's not our fault: "I know the report was due yesterday, but Frank didn't get me the statistics until this morning." If a household chore is left undone, we quickly look to our other family members to determine who is responsible. For every flaw we see around us, we usually search for someone to blame, hoping to exonerate ourselves by making sure that the one who failed is properly identified and punished.

Another reason we seek to blame others is that our success often depends on their contribution. Their failure is a threat to us. When the failure of another blocks our goal of success, we usually respond by defending ourselves and blaming them, often using condemnation to manipulate them to improve their performance. Blaming others also helps put a safe distance between their failure and our fragile self-worth.

Whether our accusations are focused on ourselves or others, we all have a tendency to believe that someone has to take the blame. When Ellen discovered that her fifteen-year-old daughter was pregnant, she went a week without sleep, tossing and turning, trying to determine who was at fault. Was it her daughter, who had brought this reproach on the family, or was she to blame for failing as a mother? All Ellen knew was that someone had to take responsibility for the crisis.

Rather than being objective and looking for a solid, biblical solution to our problems, we often resort to either accusing someone else or berating ourselves.

Sometimes, we blame others to make ourselves feel better. By blaming someone else who failed, we feel superior. In fact, the higher the position of the one who failed (parent, boss, pastor, etc.), the farther they fall, and often, the better we feel. This desire to be superior, to be "one up" on someone, is at the root of gossip.

In other situations, however, just the opposite is true. When a parent fails, a child usually accepts the blame for that failure. Even as adults, we may readily assume blame in our relationships with those in authority. We have much invested in supporting those we depend upon. This is one reason why denial is so strong in abusive families. For example, one little girl said, "I never told anybody that Daddy was molesting me because I thought that somebody would take him away from our family."

How should we respond when another fails? If the person who failed is a Christian, we need to affirm God's truth about him or her: *He (or she) is deeply loved, completely forgiven, fully pleasing, and totally accepted by God, and complete in Christ.* This perspective can eventually change our condemning attitude to one of love and a desire to help. By believing these truths, we will gradually be able to love this person just as God loves us (1 John 4:11), forgive him or her just as God has forgiven us (Eph. 4:32), and accept him or her just as God has accepted us (Rom. 15:7). This does not mean that we will become blind to the faults or failures of others. We will continue to see them, but our response to them will change considerably over time, from condemnation to compassion. As we depend less on other people for our self-worth, their sins and mistakes will become less of a threat to us, and we will desire to help them instead of being compelled to punish them.

But what about our response to unbelievers? Although they haven't yet trusted in the cross of Christ for the removal of their condemnation before God, Jesus was very clear about how we are to treat them. In Matt. 22:37, 39, He told His disciples to *love the Lord your God, with all your heart, and with all your soul, and with all your mind,* and to *love your neighbor* (both believers and unbelievers) *as yourself.* Jesus was even more specific in Luke 6:27-28. He said, *But I say to you who hear, love your enemies, do good to those who hate you, bless those who curse you, pray for those who mistreat you.* Christ didn't come to love and die for the lovely, righteous people of the world. If He had, we would all be in trouble! Instead, He came to love and die for the unrighteous, the inconsiderate, and the selfish. As we grow in our understanding of His love for us, and continue to grasp that He has rescued us from the righteous condemnation we deserve because of our sins, we will gradually become more patient and kind to others when they fail. It can be very helpful if we compare the failure or sin of others with our sin that Christ died to forgive: *There is nothing that anyone can do to me that can compare with my sin of rebellion that Christ has completely forgiven.* That should give us a lot of perspective!

We tend to make two major errors when we punish others for their failures. The first is that we condemn people not only for genuine sin, but also for their mistakes. When people who have tried their best fail, they do not need our biting blame. They need our love and encouragement. Again, we often tend to blame others because their actions (whether they reflect overt disobedience or honest mistakes) make us look like failures, and our own failure is unacceptable to us. Husband–wife, parent–child, and employer–employee relationships are especially vulnerable to one's being threatened by the failure of another. A wife gets angry with her husband for his not-so-funny joke at an important dinner party; a parent erupts at a child for accidentally spilling milk; a manager scowls at an employee because an error in the employee's calculations has made him look foolish to his supervisor. People generally experience difficulty in dealing with their *sins*; let's not compound their problems by condemning them for their *mistakes*.

A second major error we often make by condemning others is believing that we are godly agents of condemnation. Unable to tolerate injustice, we seem to possess a great need to balance the scales of right and wrong. We are correct in recognizing that sin is reprehensible and deserves condemnation; yet, we have not been licensed by God to punish others for their sins. Judgment is God's responsibility, not man's.

Jesus dealt specifically with this issue when several men decided to stone a woman caught in adultery. He told them that the person without sin should throw the first stone. Beginning with the eldest, all of the accusers walked away as they remembered their own sins (John 8:3-9). In light of their own sinfulness, they no longer saw fit to condemn the sins of another.

As this incident clearly illustrates, we should leave righteous condemnation and punishment in the hands of the One worthy of the responsibility. Our response should be love, affirmation, and possibly, compassionate correction.

When others offend or insult us, should we tell them that they have made us angry or hurt our feelings? This question can be difficult to answer. Some psychologists tell us that we should vent all of our emotions because repression is unhealthy. Others tell us that our emotions will always be positive and controlled if we are truly walking with the Lord. We should avoid both of these extremes. Venting our anger uncontrollably is not a healthy solution, but neither is continued repression and denial.

We need a safe environment to express our emotions: a good friend or counselor who will help us get in touch with our true feelings, which we may have suppressed for years. We can also learn to express ourselves fully to the Lord and tell Him our true feelings, fears, hopes, and dreams. (The Psalms are filled with honest expressions of anger, pain, confusion, hope, and faith.) In this safe environment, we can slowly learn how to communicate appropriately with those who have hurt us. This requires wisdom because each situation and each person often requires a different form of communication.

As we learn to relate appropriately with those who have hurt or injured us in some way, we will begin to develop a healthy sense of assertiveness—an important component in shaping other people's behavior toward us. For example, if others are rude, but never realize it because we passively accept their behavior in an attempt to avoid upsetting them, at least two things usually happen: We develop resentment toward them, and they never have to come to terms with their negative impact on others. They then miss an important opportunity to change, and we effectually prolong their hurtful behavior. There are appropriate and inappropriate ways of communicating our sense of anger or resentment to others, but these feelings need to be spoken—for their benefit and for ours.

We also need to remember that learning how to express our feelings appropriately is a *process*. We can't expect to respond perfectly to everyone. It takes time to express years of repressed pain. It also takes time to learn how to respond firmly and clearly. Be patient with yourself.

We have a choice in our response to failure: We can condemn or we can learn. All of us fail, but this doesn't mean that we are failures. We need to understand that failing can be a step toward maturity, not a permanent blot on our self-esteem. Like children first learning to walk, we all stumble and fall. And, just like children, we can pick ourselves up and begin again. We don't have to allow failure to prevent us from being used by God.

There have been many times in my life when I felt that God was going to punish me by causing me to lose all that I had, either because I'd done something I shouldn't have, or because I'd failed to do something I should have. This erroneous perception of God has driven me away from Him on many occasions when I've needed Him most, and is completely contrary to the One whom Paul described as *the Father of mercies and God of all comfort* (2 Cor. 1:3).

If we have trusted Christ for our salvation, God has forgiven us, and wants us to experience His forgiveness on a daily basis. Moses was a murderer, but God forgave him and used him to deliver Israel from Egypt. David was an adulterer and a murderer, but God forgave him and made him a great king. Peter denied the Lord, but God forgave him, and Peter became a leader in the Church. God rejoices when His children learn to accept His forgiveness, pick themselves up, and walk after they have stumbled. But we must also learn to forgive ourselves. Rather than viewing our weaknesses as a threat to our self-esteem, it is God's desire that they compel us to move forward in our relationship with Him. As the author of Hebrews wrote:

> *Therefore, since we have a great high priest who has gone through the heavens, Jesus the Son of God, let us hold firmly to the faith we profess.*
>
> *For we do not have a high priest who is unable to sympathize with our weaknesses, but we have one who has been tempted in every way, just as we are—yet was without sin.*
>
> *Let us then approach the throne of grace with confidence, so that we may receive mercy and find grace to help us in our time of need.*
>
> Heb. 4:14-16, NIV

Some of us have a tendency to perceive of Jesus as our friend, and God as a harsh disciplinarian. Yet the author of Hebrews described Jesus as *the radiance of [God's] glory and the exact representation of His nature* (Heb. 1:3).

Studying passages like these and spending time with compassionate, forgiving Christians has enabled the Holy Spirit to reshape my perception of God over the years. I continue to experience remorse when I fail. But rather than hide from God, fearing His punishment, I more often approach Him with appreciation for what His love has accomplished for me.

Both assuming and assigning blame for failure can have a number of detrimental consequences. Many psychologists today adhere to a theory called Rational Emotive Therapy. This very helpful theory states that blame is the core of most emotional disturbances. The answer, they insist, is for each of us to stop blaming ourselves and others, and learn to accept ourselves in spite of our imperfections. How right they are! Christ's death is the complete payment for sin, and we can claim His complete forgiveness and acceptance daily.

A number of emotional problems are rooted in the false belief that we must meet certain standards to be acceptable, and that the only way to deal with inadequacies is to punish ourselves and others for them. There is no way we can shoulder such a heavy burden. Our guilt will overpower us, and the weight of our failures will break us.

The false belief, *Those who fail (including myself) are unworthy of love and deserve to be punished,* is at the root of our fear of punishment and our propensity to punish others. How deeply are you affected by this lie? Take the following test to determine how great an influence it has in your life:

FEAR OF PUNISHMENT/PUNISHING OTHERS TEST

Read each of the following statements; then, from the top of the test, choose the term which best describes your response. Put the number above that term in the blank beside each statement.

1	2	3	4	5	6	7
Always	Very Often	Often	Sometimes	Seldom	Very Seldom	Never

_____ 1. I fear what God might do to me.

_____ 2. After I fail, I worry about God's response.

_____ 3. When I see someone in a difficult situation, I wonder what he or she did to deserve it.

_____ 4. When something goes wrong, I have a tendency to think that God must be punishing me.

_____ 5. I am very hard on myself when I fail.

_____ 6. I find myself wanting to blame people when they fail.

_____ 7. I get angry with God when someone who is immoral or dishonest prospers.

_____ 8.   I am compelled to tell others when I see them doing
           wrong.
_____ 9.   I tend to focus on the faults and failures of others.
_____10.   God seems harsh to me.
_____Total (Add up the numbers you have placed in the blanks.)

Interpretation of Score

If your score is...

57-70

God has apparently given you a very strong appreciation for His
unconditional love and acceptance. You seem to be freed from the fear of
punishment that plagues most people. (Some people who score this high
are either greatly deceived, or have become callous to their emotions as a
way to suppress pain.)

47-56

The fear of punishment and the compulsion to punish others control
your responses rarely or only in certain situations. Again, the only
exceptions are those who are not honest with themselves.

37-46

When you experience emotional problems, they may tend to relate
to a fear of punishment or to an inner urge to punish others. Upon
reflection, you will probably relate many of your previous decisions to this
fear. Many of your future decisions will also be affected by the fear of
punishment and/or the compulsion to punish others unless you take direct
action to overcome these tendencies.

27-36

The fear of punishment forms a general backdrop to your life. There
are probably few days that you are not affected in some way by the fear of
punishment and the propensity to blame others. Unfortunately, this robs
you of the joy and peace your salvation is meant to bring.

0-26

Experiences of punishment dominate your memory, and you probably have suffered a great deal of depression as a result of them. These problems will remain until some definitive plan is followed. In other words, this condition will not simply disappear; time alone cannot heal your pain. You need to experience deep healing in your self-concept, in your relationship with God, and in your relationships with others.

EFFECTS OF THE FEAR OF PUNISHMENT AND THE COMPULSION TO PUNISH OTHERS

The logical result of Satan's deception, *Self-worth = Performance + Others' Opinions*, is fear—the fear of failure, rejection, and punishment. When we base our security and value on how well we perform and how we want others to perceive us, failure poses a tremendous threat to us. When threatened, we will often withdraw from the source of our fear and/or become very controlling of ourselves and others. For example, in an attempt to avoid failure, we may adhere to a fairly rigid schedule in which we're fairly certain of success, and avoid those activities which are less promising. Because we often perceive those closest to us as a reflection of ourselves, and are consequently threatened by their failures, we are likely to try to control their behavior as well. If we have also determined that those who fail deserve to be punished, we will tend to victimize ourselves and/or others for virtually any wrongdoing.

Because of our insecurity, some of us are so self-protective that we are rarely able to perceive of ourselves as being in the wrong. We may be quick to pinpoint—and condemn—the weaknesses of others, but in our own self-evaluation, we may be effectually blind to faults and frailties. This attitude may prompt us to turn others (who are "more needy") to God, but may prevent us from seeking Him because of our frequent inability to see our need for Him, or because when we do fail, we may believe that the fault is His.

Some of us may fall on the other end of the spectrum. We may be so absorbed in our performance and so demanding of ourselves that when failure enters our circumstances, we believe that we are solely responsible. Rather than laying blame on someone else, we inflict punishment on ourselves and protect those who hurt us by explaining their deficiencies: *She didn't mean what she said. I'm sure that he loves me; he just has a hard time showing it.* If we have a tendency to punish ourselves for failures, we may believe that we must feel remorse for a certain length of time before we can experience peace and joy again. In a twisted form of self-motivation, we may think that if we condemn ourselves enough, then perhaps we won't fail again.

Somewhere in the middle of this spectrum are those of us who are so hard on ourselves that we project our self-condemning attitude onto others. Passing judgment on others may be a response to our great need for consistency and justice. If we are going to punish failure in ourselves, we reason, then we must be consistent and punish failure in others. Insisting on justice, we may also take it upon ourselves to be God's instrument of correction. We normally don't like to see others getting away with something that they should be punished for (or perhaps, that we wish we could do ourselves).

Finally, there are those of us who determine that because punishment is inevitable, we may as well "live it up" and enjoy our sin before the Judgment comes.

The fear of punishment and the propensity to punish others can affect our lives in many ways. The following provides a brief description of common problems which often result from this deception:

Self-Induced Punishment

Many of us operate on the theory that if we are hard enough on ourselves, then God won't have to punish us. We fail to realize that God disciplines us in love and never punishes us in anger. Because God loves us unconditionally and does not punish us, we don't need to punish ourselves.

Bitterness

If we believe that God and others are always punishing us, we will soon become very angry. Harboring anger and continually questioning God's motives result in deep bitterness and pessimism.

Passivity

Fear of punishment is at the root of one of the most common problems in our society: passivity. *Passivity* is the neglect of our minds, time, gifts, or talents through inaction. God intends for us to actively cooperate with Him, but fear can have an immobilizing effect on our will. Passivity results in a dull life, avoiding risks, and missing opportunities.

Punishing Others

Our specific response to the failure of others depends on several factors: our personalities, the nature of their failure, and how their failure reflects on us (*His mistake makes me look like I'm dumb*, or ...*a bad parent*, or ...*a poor leader*, or ...*a rotten employee*). Our condemnation of those who fail may take the form of verbal abuse, physical abuse, nagging criticism, withholding appreciation and affection, or ignoring them. All of these responses are usually designed to "make them pay for what they did."

The fear of punishment and the desire to punish others can be overcome by realizing that Christ has borne the punishment we deserve. His motives toward us are loving and kind. His discipline is designed to correct us and protect us from the destruction of sin, not to punish us.

GOD'S ANSWER: PROPITIATION

When Christ died on the cross, He was our substitute. He took upon Himself the righteous wrath of God that we deserved. The depth of God's love for us is revealed by the extremity of His actions for us: the holy Son of God became a man and died a horrible death in our place. Two passages state this eloquently. The first was written by Isaiah, who anticipated the coming of Christ:

Surely our griefs He Himself bore, and our sorrows He carried; yet we ourselves esteemed Him stricken, smitten of God, and afflicted.

But He was pierced through for our transgressions, He was crushed for our iniquities; the chastening for our well-being fell upon Him, and by His scourging we are healed.

All of us like sheep have gone astray, each of us has turned to his own way; but the Lord has caused the iniquity of us all to fall on Him.

Is. 53:4-6

And from the New Testament:

By this the love of God was manifested in us, that God has sent His only begotten Son into the world so that we might live through Him.

In this is love, not that we loved God, but that He loved us and sent His Son to be the propitiation for our sins.

Beloved, if God so loved us, we also ought to love one another.

1 John 4:9-11

Propitiation means that the wrath of someone who has been unjustly wronged has been satisfied. It is an act that soothes hostility and satisfies the need for vengeance. Providing His only begotten Son as the propitiation for our sin was the greatest possible demonstration of God's love for man.

To understand God's wondrous provision of propitiation, it is helpful to remember what He has endured from mankind. From Adam and Eve's sin in the Garden of Eden to the obvious depravity we see in our world today, human history is mainly the story of greed, hatred, lust, and pride—evidence of man's wanton rebellion against the God of love and peace. If not done with a desire to glorify Him, even our "good" deeds are like filthy garments to God (Is. 64:6).

Our sin deserves the righteous wrath of God. He is the Almighty, the rightful judge of the universe. He is absolutely holy and perfect. *God is light, and in Him there is no darkness at all* (1 John 1:5). Because of these attributes, God cannot overlook sin, nor can He compromise by accepting sinful behavior. For God to condone even one sin would defile His holiness like smearing a white satin wedding gown with black tar.

Because He is holy, God's aversion to sin is manifested in righteous anger. However, God is not only righteously indignant about sin, He is also infinitely loving. In His holiness, God condemns sin, but in the most awesome example of love the world has ever seen, He ordained that His Son would die to pay for our sins. God sacrificed the sinless, perfect Savior to turn away, *to propitiate*, His great wrath.

And for whom did Christ die? Was it for the saints who honored Him? Was it for a world that appreciated His sinless life and worshipped Him? No! Christ died for *us*, while we were yet in rebellion against Him:

> *For while we were still helpless, at the right time Christ died for the ungodly.*
>
> *For one will hardly die for a righteous man; though perhaps for the good man someone would dare even to die.*
>
> *But God demonstrates His own love toward us, in that while we were yet sinners, Christ died for us.*
>
> *Much more then, having now been justified by His blood, we shall be saved from the wrath of God through Him.*
>
> *For if while we were enemies, we were reconciled to God through the death of His Son, much more, having been reconciled, we shall be saved by His life.*
>
> *And not only this, but we also exult in God through our Lord Jesus Christ, through whom we have now received the reconciliation.*
>
> Rom. 5:6-11

Who can measure the fathomless depth of love that sent Christ to the cross? While we were the enemies of God, Christ averted the wrath we deserved so that we might become the sons of God.

What can we say of our holy heavenly Father? Surely, He did not escape seeing Christ's mistreatment at the hands of sinful men—the scourgings, the humiliation, the beatings. Surely, He who spoke the world into being could have delivered Christ from the entire ordeal. And yet, the God of heaven peered down through time and saw you and me. Though we were His enemies, He loved us and longed to rescue us from our sins, and designated the sinless Christ to become our substitute. Only Christ could avert God's righteous wrath against sin, so in love, the Father kept silent as Jesus hung from the cross. All of His anger, all of the wrath we would ever deserve, was poured upon Christ, and Christ became sin for us (2 Cor. 5:21). Because he paid the penalty for our sins, and God's wrath was avenged, God no longer looks upon us through the eyes of judgment, but instead, He now lavishes His love upon us. The Scriptures teach that absolutely nothing can separate us from God's love (Rom. 8:38-39). He has adopted us into a tender, intimate, and powerful relationship with Him (Rom. 8:15).

Because we are His children, performance is no longer the basis of our worth. We are unconditionally and deeply loved by God, and we can live by faith in His grace. We were spiritually dead, but the Lord has made us alive and has given us the high status of sonship to the Almighty God. It will take all of eternity to comprehend the wealth of His love and grace. Paul explains this incomprehensible gift this way:

> *But God, being rich in mercy, because of His great love with which He loved us,*
> *even when we were dead in our transgressions, made us alive together with Christ (by grace you have been saved),*
> *and raised us up with Him, and seated us with Him in the heavenly places, in Christ Jesus,*

> *in order that in the ages to come He might show the*
> *surpassing riches of His grace in kindness toward us in Christ*
> *Jesus.*
>
> *For by grace you have been saved through faith; and that*
> *not of yourselves, it is the gift of God;*
>
> > *not as a result of works, that no one should boast.*
> >
> > Eph. 2:4-9

Propitiation, then, means that Christ has satisfied the holy wrath of God through His payment for sin. There was only one reason for Him to do this: He loves us; infinitely, eternally, unconditionally, irrevocably, He loves us. God the Father loves us with the love of a father, reaching to snatch us from harm. God the Son loves us with the love of a brother, laying down His life for us. He alone has turned away God's wrath from us. There is nothing we can do, no amount of good deeds we can accomplish, and no religious ceremonies we can perform that can pay for our sins. Instead, Christ has conclusively paid for them so that we can escape eternal condemnation and experience His love and purposes both now and forever.

Christ not only paid for our sins at one point in time, but continues to love us and teach us day after day. We have a weapon to use against Satan as he attacks us with doubts about God's love for us. Our weapon is the fact that Christ took our punishment upon Himself at Calvary. We no longer have to fear punishment for our sins because Christ paid for them all—past, present, and future. This tremendous truth of propitiation clearly demonstrates that we are truly and deeply loved by God. His perfect love casts out all fear as we allow it to flood our hearts (1 John 4:18).

A BEGINNING EXERCISE

How do we begin to experience freedom from Satan's lie: *Those who fail are unworthy of love and deserve to be punished*? We will be increasingly freed as we understand and apply the truth of propitiation in the context of loving and supportive relationships, where we can express ourselves honestly and receive both the warmth of affirmation and the challenge of God's Word.

The Scriptures indicate that Satan accuses believers of being unworthy of God's grace. It is his desire that we cower under the fear of punishment. Consider this passage from Rev. 12:10-11:

> *And I heard a loud voice in heaven, saying, "Now the salvation, and the power, and the authority of His Christ have come, for the accuser of our brethren has been thrown down, who accuses them before our God day and night.*
>
> *And they overcame him because of the blood of the Lamb and because of the word of their testimony, and they did not love their life even to death.*

How are we to overcome Satan, the accuser, and experience our acceptance in Christ? According to this passage of Scripture, there is only one way: by the sacrificial blood of Christ on the cross, the blood of the Lamb. To do this, we must first stop trying to overcome our feelings of condemnation and failure by penitent actions. Defending ourselves or trying to pay for our sins by our actions leads only to a guilt-and-penance spiral because we can never do enough on our own to justify our sins.

There have been times when I thought that I couldn't feel forgiven until I had experienced remorse about my sin for a certain period of time. These occasions led to depression, because I could hardly complete my penance for one sin before I had sinned again. Then, I would have to feel badly about *that* for a period of time, only to sin again...and again...and again...and....

Eventually, I began to realize that I had one of three options: I could continue trying to make up for my sin by mourning over it for however long it seemed necessary (although that wasn't getting me very far); I could try to deny that I had sinned (even though I knew that I had); or I could give up on the idea of using my guilt as a form of penance, and trust in Christ's forgiveness. Initially, of course, these options were not as clear as they've become with time and reflection.

No matter how much we do to make up for our sin, we will continue to feel guilty and believe that we need to do more unless we resist Satan, the accuser of the brethren. This can only be accomplished because Christ's blood has completely paid for our sins and delivered us from guilt.

Secondly, we need to verbalize what the blood of Christ has done for us: *We are deeply loved, completely forgiven, fully pleasing, totally accepted, and complete in Christ.*

As the Bible says in Rev. 12:11, we should not love our lives (the excitement, comfort, prestige, and status) to the point of spiritual deadness. Love for the world and its pleasures renders us spiritually impotent. We must decide that our minds are no longer the source of truth, and instead gain our knowledge, wisdom, and direction from the Scriptures. There are two practical steps that will help make these truths a reality in our lives:

1. On one side of a 3x5 card, write the following:
    Because of Christ and His redemption, I am completely forgiven and fully pleasing to God. I am totally accepted by God.

2. On the other side of the card, write the words of Rom. 5:1 and Col. 1:21-22.

Carry this card with you for the next twenty-eight days. Every time you get something to drink, or do some other routine activity, look at it and remind yourself of what Christ has done for you. This exercise will help you develop a habit of reflecting on these liberating truths. As you read and memorize these statements and passages, think about how they apply to you. Memorization and application of these truths will have profound effects on your life as your mind is slowly transformed by God's Word.

Nine
Shame

When we base our self-worth on past failures, dissatisfaction with personal appearance, or bad habits, we often develop a fourth false belief: *I am what I am. I cannot change. I am hopeless.* This lie binds people to the hopeless pessimism associated with poor self-esteem.

"I just can't help myself," some people say. "That's the way I've always been, and that's the way I'll always be. You can't teach an old dog new tricks." We assume that others should have low expectations of us, too. "You know I can't do any better than that. What do you expect?"

If we excuse our failures with an attitude of hopelessness too often, our personality can become glued to them. Our self-image becomes no more than a reflection of our past.

When Leslie approached Janet about serving a term as president of the Ladies' Auxiliary, Janet's outward poise and confidence vanished.

"Are you serious?" she stuttered. "You know I've never been a leader, and have never even gotten along well with people. No, no, I'd simply be an embarrassment to you. No, I can't do it, don't you see?"

Janet was suffering from low self-esteem. Her opinions of herself were based on her past failures, and those failures kept her from enjoying new experiences.

A young man named Jeff once questioned me when I told him that he needed to separate his past from the present, and that no natural law dictated his having to remain the same individual he had always been. I told Jeff that he could change, that he could rise above his past and build a new life for himself.

"But how?" Jeff asked. "I'm more of a realist than that. I know myself. I know what I've done and who I am. I've tried to change, but it hasn't worked. I've given up now."

I explained to Jeff that he needed a new perspective, not just new efforts based on his old, pessimistic attitude. He needed to develop a new self-concept based on the unconditional love and acceptance of God. Both Jeff's past failures and God's unconditional love were realities, but the question was which one Jeff would value more. If he continued to value his failures, he would continue to be absorbed in self-pity. Instead, he needed to be honest. He needed someone he could talk to openly, so that he could express his feelings without the fear of being rejected. And he needed to be encouraged to study and apply the truths of God's Word. As he persisted in this process, his sense of self-worth would begin to change. In addition to a changed self-worth, he would eventually experience changes in every area of his life: his goals, his relationships, and his outlook.

Too often, our self-image rests solely on an evaluation of our past behavior, being measured only through a memory. Day after day, year after year, we tend to build our personalities upon the rubble of yesterday's personal disappointments.

Perhaps we find some strange kind of comfort in our personal failings. Perhaps there is some security in accepting ourselves as much less than we can become. That minimizes the risk of failure. Certainly, if we expect little from ourselves we will seldom be disappointed!

But nothing forces us to remain in the mold of the past. By the grace and power of God, we can change! We can persevere and overcome! No one forces us to keep shifting our feet in the muck of old failures. We can dare to accept the challenge of building a new life.

Dr. Paul Tournier once compared life to a man hanging from a trapeze. The trapeze bar was the man's security, his pattern of existence, his lifestyle. Then God swung another trapeze into the man's view, and he faced a perplexing dilemma. Should he relinquish his past? Should he reach for the new bar? The moment of truth came, Dr. Tournier explained, when the man realized that to grab onto the new bar, he must release the old one.

Our past relationships may involve the intense pain of neglect, abuse, and manipulation, but if we do not begin the process of healing, we will be unable to experience the joy, challenge, and yes, the potential for failure in the present.

I have struggled with this process of change for the greater part of my life. It may have been that I was raised in a poor family. It may have been that while I was growing up, I often felt very awkward. It may have been that there were some inadequacies in my home life. For whatever reasons, I grew up with a sense of shame about myself and my circumstances.

As I've mentioned previously, I often felt inadequate during my childhood. I had the impression that I just didn't measure up. Others might not have thought I felt this way, but my sense of inadequacy was often intense.

Being exceptionally tall and lanky, I was uncomfortable with the way I looked, and felt out of place among my peers. My feelings of inferiority prevented me from pursuing dating relationships for a number of years. The threat of potential rejection prompted me to withdraw from social gatherings, preferring instead to spend time with the few friends I felt most comfortable with.

The truth that I am deeply loved, fully pleasing, and totally accepted by the God of the universe has taken me a lifetime to comprehend. But gradually, by studying God's Word and by experiencing loving relationships with other believers who genuinely care for me and appreciate me, I have continued to gain a better understanding of the way God values me. This has improved my sense of self-worth considerably.

Many of my past memories are still painful for me, and I imagine they always will be. But through Christ, my present attitude about myself is continually changing. Knowing that I have no reason to feel ashamed has motivated me to pursue a number of challenges that I wouldn't have even considered pursuing a number of years ago. In the process, I have experienced failure and success. God has used each instance to teach me that despite my circumstances, my worth is secure in Him.

We need to be honest about the pain, the anger, the disappointment, and the loneliness of our past. We need to put ourselves in relationships that will encourage us to feel what we may have suppressed for many years. This will enable us to begin (or continue) to experience hope, and eventually, healing. Change is possible, but it is a process.

Does this seem strange? Does it seem difficult? We may have difficulty relinquishing what is familiar (though painful) for what is unfamiliar because our fear of the unknown often seems stronger than the pain of a poor self-concept. It seems right to hang on. Proverbs 16:25 says, *There is a way which seems right to a man, but its end is the way of death.*

Any change in our behavior requires a release from our old self-concept, which is often founded in failure and the expectations of others. We need to learn how to relate to ourselves in a new way. To accomplish this, we must begin to base our self-worth on God's opinion of us and trust in His Spirit to accomplish change in our lives. Then, and only then, can we overcome Satan's deception that holds sway over our self-perception and behavior.

By believing Satan's lie, *I am what I am, I cannot change, I am hopeless,* we become vulnerable to pessimism and a poor self-concept. Take the test on the following page to determine how strongly you are affected by this false belief:

SHAME TEST

Read each of the following statements; then, choose the term from the top of the test which best describes your response. Put the number above that term in the blank beside each statement.

1	2	3	4	5	6	7
Always	Very Often	Often	Sometimes	Seldom	Very Seldom	Never

_____ 1.   I often think about past failures or experiences of rejection.

_____ 2.   There are certain things about my past which I cannot recall without experiencing strong, painful emotions (i.e. guilt, shame, anger, fear, etc.).

_____ 3.   I seem to make the same mistakes over and over again.

_____ 4.   There are certain aspects of my character that I want to change, but I don't believe I can ever successfully do so.

_____ 5.   I feel inferior.

_____ 6.   There are aspects of my appearance that I cannot accept.

_____ 7.   I am generally disgusted with myself.

_____ 8.   I feel that certain experiences have basically ruined my life.

_____ 9.   I perceive of myself as an immoral person.

_____10.   I feel that I have lost the opportunity to experience a complete and wonderful life.

_____ Total (Add up the numbers you have placed in the blanks.)

Interpretation of Score

If your score is...

57-70

God has apparently given you a very strong appreciation for His love and unconditional acceptance. You seem to be freed from the shame that plagues most people. (Some people who score this high are either greatly deceived, or have become callous to their emotions as a way to suppress pain.)

47-56

Shame controls your responses rarely or only in certain situations. Again, the exceptions are those who are not honest with themselves.

37-46

When you experience emotional problems, they may relate to a sense of shame. Upon reflection, you will probably relate many of your previous decisions to feelings of worthlessness. Many of your future decisions will also be affected by low self-esteem unless you take direct action to overcome it.

27-36

Shame forms a generally negative backdrop to your life. There are probably few days that you are not affected in some way by shame. Unfortunately, this robs you of the joy and peace your salvation was meant to bring.

0-26

Experiences of shame dominate your memory, and have probably resulted in a great deal of depression. These problems will remain until some definitive action is taken. In other words, this condition will not simply disappear one day; time alone cannot heal your pain. You need to experience deep healing in your self-concept, in your relationship with God, and in your relationships with others.

EFFECTS OF SHAME

Susan was the product of heartless parents. Although she was a beautiful girl with dark brown eyes and long, silky hair, Susan never seemed quite as confident or as outgoing as her brothers and sisters. One reason for this was that by her eighth birthday, Susan had been approached by her father for sexual favors. Overcome by the shame this caused her, Susan withdrew from others and looked for an escape.

By the time she was sixteen, Susan was addicted to alcohol and drugs, and was frequently stealing as well as selling her body for money. She had accepted the belief that she was nothing more than sexual merchandise. Although she was ashamed of her lifestyle and wanted to change, she saw no way out. The only people who didn't seem to reject her were the ones who used her. She was not only ashamed, but was also trapped and alone.

Unlike Susan, Diana was raised by Christian parents. She had grown up in a conservative Protestant church and was very active in its youth group. Diana was diligent in witnessing to her friends at school, and her actions were always an example to those around her.

Unfortunately, Diana made a mistake one night that changed her life. Alone for the evening, she and her boyfriend went too far. Shocked and ashamed by their actions, they both agreed that they must admit the incident to their parents. Tearfully, Diana confided in her mother, looking for understanding and support. But Diana's mother lost control and bitterly told her how ashamed and disappointed she was. Diana's father couldn't believe what she had done, and refused even to speak to her.

Her relationship with her parents continued to worsen and six months later, Diana left home. Heartbroken and overcome by shame, she turned to her boyfriend. Soon, they began sleeping together regularly, and both began using drugs. Believing that her parents would never accept her again, Diana sought acceptance in the only way she knew how.

Both Susan and Diana suffered from the devastating effects of shame. Shame often engulfs us when a flaw in our performance is so important, so overpowering, or so disappointing to us that it creates a permanently negative opinion about our self-worth. Others may not know of our failure, but we do. We may only imagine their rejection, but real or imagined, the pain resulting from it cripples our confidence and hope.

Shame usually results in guilt and self-deprecation, but it can also lead us to search for God and His answers. Our inner, undeniable need for personal significance was created to make us search for Him. He alone can fulfill our deep need. In Him, we find peace, acceptance, and love. Through Him, we find the courage and power to develop into the men and women He intends us to be. Although Satan wants to convince us that we will always be prisoners of our failures and past experiences, by God's grace we can be freed from the guilt of our past, and experience a renewed purpose for our lives.

Shame can have powerful effects on our esteem, and it can manifest itself in many ways. The following is a brief list of common problems associated with shame:

Inferiority

By definition, *shame* is a deep sense of inferiority. Feelings of inferiority can result from prolonged patterns of failure, or they can stem from only one or two haunting instances. Either way, they can destroy our self-worth, and as a result, adversely affect our emotions and behavior. These perceptions of ourselves aren't easily altered, but they can change through honesty, the affirmation of others, the truths of God's Word, the power and encouragement of the Holy Spirit, and time. Because of Christ's redemption, we are worthy, forgiven, loved, accepted, and complete in Him.

Habitually Destructive Behavior

We often behave in a manner that is consistent with our perception of ourselves. Therefore, seeing ourselves through the eyes of shame usually results in a pessimistic outlook on life and a lifestyle of destructive behavior.

Self-Pity

Shame often prompts us to view ourselves as victims. Consequently, whether we blame others or condemn ourselves for our actions, we sink into the depths of feeling sorry for ourselves.

Passivity

Some of us try to compensate for gnawing feelings of shame through passivity, refusing to invest any part of ourselves in relationships and responsibilities. We may be compulsive perfectionists in some areas of our lives, but may avoid taking risks in relationships or circumstances. We may tend to become engrossed in peripheral activities (clipping coupons, cleaning the kitchen, filing papers, reading magazines), so that we are "too busy" to experience the reality of relationships and situations.

Isolation and Withdrawal

Isolation is often a corollary of passivity. Avoiding both the risks of rejection and failure, some of us withdraw from virtually all meaningful interaction. We develop facades, so that nobody can see our hurt. We may be socially active, but may not allow anyone to get really close to us. We are often afraid that if people *really* knew us, we would again experience hurt and rejection. Our deep sense of shame leads us to withdraw from others, feel isolated, and experience the pain of loneliness.

Loss of Creativity

When we are ashamed of ourselves over a period of time, the cutting edge of our creativity atrophies. We tend to become so preoccupied with our own inferiority that we are unable to come up with new ideas. Often believing that whatever we attempt will fail, we may choose to avoid doing anything that isn't a proven success and relatively risk-free.

Codependent Relationships

In an attempt to overcome their sense of shame, many people become *codependent*; that is, they depend on being needed by a family member or friend who has an addictive problem or compulsion. Codependents thus develop a need to "rescue" and take care of others. This caretaking is the codependent's subconscious way of trying to gain personal significance. Such attempts usually backfire, however, because dependent persons often use shame to manipulate the codependent. A frequent ploy is to tell the codependent that he or she is being "selfish" for taking care of personal affairs rather than those of the dependent person. This locks the codependent into a hopeless pattern of rescuing to gain approval and feeling ashamed because of his or her inability to develop a sense of personal value, regardless of how hard he or she tries to do so.

Despising Our Appearance

Beauty is highly valued in our society. Television commercials and programs, magazine ads and billboards all convey the message that beauty is to be prized. But very few of us compare to the beautiful people we see in these ads and programs, and most of us are ashamed of at least one aspect of our appearance. We spend hundreds of dollars and an inestimable amount of time and worry covering up or altering our skin, eyes, teeth, faces, noses, thighs, and scalps, refusing to believe that God, in His sovereignty and love, gave us the features He wants us to have.

GOD'S ANSWER: REGENERATION

Perhaps no passage in the Bible better illustrates God's regeneration than the story of Zaccheus in Luke 19:1-10. Zaccheus was a tax collector, despised by the people for overtaxing their meager earnings. There were few in the Roman world more despicable than tax collectors, who obtained their wealth at the expense of others.

One day, Zaccheus learned that Jesus was visiting his town, and climbed a sycamore tree to get a good look at the man who reportedly loved even sinners and outcasts. Jesus saw him in the tree, and to the astonishment of all—including Zaccheus—invited him to come down, and then went to his house to eat with him!

During dinner, Zaccheus experienced the unconditional love and acceptance of Christ. As a result, he became a different person. His self-concept was radically changed from a swindling, loathsome tax collector to a person who knew he was loved by God. His actions reflected this dramatic change. He pledged to repent of his sins and repay fourfold those he had swindled. He also promised to give half of his possessions to the poor. Through Christ, Zaccheus developed a new self-concept, new values, new goals, and new behavior.

Regeneration is not a self-improvement program, nor is it a clean-up campaign for our sinful natures. *Regeneration* is nothing less than the impartation of new life. As Paul stated in Eph. 2:5, we were once dead in our sins, but have since been made alive in Christ.

Paul also wrote about this incredible transformation process in his letter to the young pastor, Titus:

> *For we also once were foolish ourselves, disobedient, deceived, enslaved to various lusts and pleasures, spending our life in malice and envy, hateful, hating one another.*
>
> *But when the kindness of God our Savior and His love for mankind appeared,*
>
> *He saved us, not on the basis of deeds which we have done in righteousness, but according to His mercy, by the washing of regeneration and renewing by the Holy Spirit,*
>
> *whom He poured out upon us richly through Jesus Christ our Savior,*

*that being justified by His grace we might be made heirs
according to the hope of eternal life.*

Titus 3:3-7

Regeneration is the renewing work of the Holy Spirit that literally makes each believer a new person at the moment he or she trusts Christ as Savior.

In that wondrous, miraculous moment, we experience more than swapping one set of standards for another. We experience what Jesus called a new birth (John 3:3-6), a Spirit-wrought renewal of the human spirit, a transforming resuscitation which takes place so that the Spirit is alive within us (Rom. 8:10).

Through the gift of God's grace, we are spiritually alive, forgiven, and complete in Him. Paul wrote the Colossian Christians:

For in Him (Christ) *all the fullness of Deity dwells in bodily form,*
and in Him you have been made complete, and He is the head over all rule and authority.

Col. 2:9-10

In the church at Colossae, false teachers taught that "completeness" came through a combination of philosophy, good works, other religions, and Christ. Paul's clear message was that we are made complete *through Christ alone.* To attempt to find completeness through any other source, including success, the approval of others, prestige, or appearance, is to be taken captive through philosophy and empty deception (Col. 2:8). Nothing can add to the death of Christ to pay for our sins and the resurrection of Christ to give us new life. We are complete because Christ has forgiven us and given us life—the capacity for growth and change.

According to the theologian, Louis Berkhof, "Regeneration consists in the implanting of the principle of the new spiritual life in man, in a radical change of the governing disposition of the soul, which, under the influence of the Holy Spirit, gives birth to a life that moves in a Godward direction. In principle this change affects the whole man: the intellect...the will...and the feelings or emotions."[1]

When we trust Christ and experience new life, forgiveness, and love, our lives will begin to change. Still, regeneration does not affect an instantaneous change in the full realm of our performance. We will continue to stumble and fall at times, but the Scriptures clearly instruct us to choose to act in ways that reflect our new lives and values in Christ. As Paul wrote the Ephesians:

> *that, in reference to your former manner of life, you lay aside the old self, which is being corrupted in accordance with the lusts of deceit,*
> *and that you be renewed in the spirit of your mind,*
> *and put on the new self, which in the likeness of God has been created in righteousness and holiness of the truth.*
>
> Eph. 4:22-24

We are to *put on*, or envelop ourselves in, this new self that progressively expresses Christian character in our attitudes and behavior. We are marvelously unique, created to reflect the character of Christ through our individual personalities and behavior. Each believer, in a different and special way, has the capability to shine forth the light of God. No two will reflect His light in exactly the same way.

The truth of regeneration can dispel the specter of the past. Our sins have been forgiven, and we now have tremendous capabilities for growth and change because we are new people with the Spirit of God living in us. Yes, when we sin, we will experience its destructive effects and the Father's discipline, but our sin will never change the truth of who we are in Christ.

When we do sin, we should follow King David's example. When Nathan confronted David about his sin of adultery with Bathsheba, David confessed his sin to the Lord (2 Sam. 12:1-13). David did not run from his sin or its consequences. He married Bathsheba, and God was merciful: He enabled Bathsheba to give birth to Solomon, the wise king of Israel. Certainly, God could have brought Solomon into the world another way, but perhaps as a message to us, He chose Bathsheba.

What a message! Confess your sins, worship God, and get on with your life. You can experience the mercy of God no matter what you've been through.

A BEGINNING EXERCISE

Satan wants us to believe the lie: *I am what I am. I cannot change. I am hopeless.*

How can you begin to experience freedom from the fear of shame? Start by looking up the following verses and reflecting on who you are in Christ. Paraphrase each of the following passages about your new life in Him:

Matt. 5:13 _____

_____

Matt. 5:14 _____

_____

Rom.1:7 _____

_____

Rom. 5:17-18 _____

_____

Rom. 8:1 _____

_____

Rom. 8:17 _____

_____

Rom. 8:37 _____

_____

2 Cor. 5:17 _____

_____

2 Cor. 5:21_____

_____

Gal. 2:20_____

_____

Eph. 1:5_____

_____

Eph. 1:7_____

_____

Eph. 2:4-6_____

_____

Eph. 2:10_____

_____

Eph. 6:10_____

_____

Col. 2:10_____

_____

Col. 3:12_____

_____

1 Pet. 1:16_____

_____

1 John 4:17_____

_____

These passages describe the stable and secure identity we have in Christ. It is our privilege to be His children; to experience His love, forgiveness, and power; and to express our appreciation of Him to others.

To summarize the last four chapters:

Because of *justification*, you are completely forgiven and fully pleasing to God. You no longer have to fear failure.

Because of *reconciliation*, you are totally accepted by God. You no longer have to fear rejection.

Because of *propitiation*, you are deeply loved by God. You no longer have to fear punishment; nor do you have to punish others.

Because of *regeneration*, you have been made brand new, complete in Christ. You no longer need to experience the pain of shame.

Ten

Obstacles to Growth

Our redemption was made complete at Calvary. When Jesus lifted up His eyes and cried, *It is finished!* (John 19:30), He told us that the provision for man's reconciliation with God was complete. Nothing more need be done, because the Word of life had been spoken to all mankind. Man needed only to hear the Word, accept it, and place his hope and trust in Christ.

But if the redemption we enjoy is complete, why do we so often fail to see the changes in our lives we long for? Why do we wrestle day after day with the same temptations, the same failings, and the same distractions we have always fought? Why can't we break free and move on toward maturity?

Christ illustrated the reasons for our lack of fruitfulness in the parable of the sower in Mark 4:3-20. In agriculture, productivity depends on the fertility of the soil, the climate, and the presence or absence of weeds. The reasons Christ gave for lack of fruit in the believer's life were: Satan's taking away the Word of God, persecution, and the worries of the world. For most of us, the worries of the world are the primary culprit for our lack of growth. Jesus described it this way:

> *And others are the ones on whom seed was sown among the thorns; these are the ones who have heard the word,*
>
> *and the worries of the world, and the deceitfulness of riches, and the desires for other things enter in and choke the word, and it becomes unfruitful.*
>
> Mark 4:18-19

In the context of honesty, affirmation, and patience, we can focus on the forgiveness we have received, and reject the deception and worldly desires that choke out the Word of life. We need to base our lives on God's Word and allow His character to be reproduced within us by the power of His Spirit:

> *And those are the ones on whom seed was sown on the good soil; and they hear the word and accept it, and bear fruit, thirty, sixty, and a hundredfold.*
>
> Mark 4:20

The moment we trust Christ, we are given *everything pertaining to life and godliness* (2 Pet. 1:2-4). Immediately, we become His sons and daughters, with all the provisions He has graciously given us. As we allow Him to reign over the affairs of our lives, He transforms our values, attitudes, and behavior so that we are able to glorify Him more and more. Of course, we are still chained to a mortal body, but we are reborn in righteousness and holiness of the truth. We have within us the Christ who has authority over Satan. Christ has triumphed over him by the power of His blood to pay for sin, and by the power of His resurrection to give new life (Col. 2:15).

Now redeemed, our rightful purpose to rule in life will only be denied if we continue to allow Satan to deceive us. If we fail to recognize our true position of sonship, and fail to exercise our new power and authority, we will remain trapped in the world's system. Satan's lies and schemes are designed to keep us from recognizing and experiencing these wonderful truths.

In order to overcome Satan's lies and begin to enjoy freedom from false beliefs, we need to have a clear understanding of what Christ has done for us through His death on the cross. The more fully we understand the implications of Christ's sacrifice, the more we will experience the freedom, motivation, and power God intends for us. God's Word is the source of truth: the truth about Christ, the cross, and redemption.

The Apostle Peter wrote that the cross is not just the beginning of Christian life, but our constant motivation to grow spiritually and to live for Christ:

> *Now for this very reason also, applying all diligence, in your faith supply moral excellence, and in your moral excellence, knowledge;*
>
> *and in your knowledge, self-control, and in your self-control, perseverance, and in your perseverance, godliness;*
>
> *and in your godliness, brotherly kindness, and in your brotherly kindness, love.*
>
> *For if these qualities are yours and are increasing, they render you neither useless nor unfruitful in the true knowledge of our Lord Jesus Christ.*
>
> *For he who lacks these qualities is blind or shortsighted, having forgotten his purification from his former sins.*
>
> 2 Pet. 1:5-9

This passage clearly teaches that the absence of spiritual growth can be traced to a lack of understanding or a failure to remember the implications of Christ's forgiveness. The cross is central to our motivation and development.

I have given you a beginning exercise for each of four false beliefs in previous chapters, but this is only a start. In the closing chapters, we'll look at the basics of renewing the heart and mind: experiencing the power of the Holy Spirit, and replacing thought patterns that tell us our worth is based on *performance plus others' opinions* with those that focus on the truths of God's unconditional love for us.

The principles in this book can be life-changing, but they are applied most readily in an environment where we are encouraged to be honest about our hurt, anger, joys, and hopes. Most of us are not very perceptive about ourselves (though we may be very perceptive about other people), and we need both the objectivity and the affirmation of others as we continue the process of application. It is also important to realize that working through these principles once is not enough. Many whom I have counseled, and many who have read this material in its previous edition, report that they have experienced dramatic growth only as they have applied these truths at an increasingly deeper level of their lives.

Let's review for a minute. The chart on the following pages depicts the contrast between the rival belief systems. Use the chart to help you when you want to determine if any particular thought is based on a lie or on God's truth. If the thought is based on a lie, learn how to confront it and overcome it with the truth of God's Word.

FALSE BELIEFS	CONSEQUENCES OF FALSE BELIEFS
I must meet certain standards in order to feel good about myself.	The fear of failure; perfectionism; being driven to succeed; manipulating others to achieve success; withdrawing from healthy risks
I must have the approval of certain others to feel good about myself.	The fear of rejection; attempting to please others at any cost; being overly sensitive to criticism; withdrawing from others to avoid disapproval
Those who fail (including myself) are unworthy of love and deserve to be punished.	The fear of punishment; propensity to punish others; blaming self and others for personal failure; withdrawing from God and fellow believers; being driven to avoid punishment
I am what I am. I cannot change. I am hopeless.	Feelings of shame, hopelessness, inferiority; passivity; loss of creativity; isolation, withdrawing from others

GOD'S SPECIFIC SOLUTION	RESULTS OF GOD'S SOLUTION
Because of justification, *I am completely forgiven and fully pleasing to God. I no longer have to fear failure.*	Increasing freedom from the fear of failure; desire to pursue the right things: Christ and His kingdom; love for Christ
Because of reconciliation, *I am totally accepted by God. I no longer have to fear rejection.*	Increasing freedom from the fear of rejection; willingness to be open and vulnerable; able to relax around others; willingness to take criticism; desire to please God no matter what others think
Because of propitiation, *I am deeply loved by God. I no longer have to fear punishment or punish others.*	Increasing freedom from the fear of punishment; patience and kindness toward others; being quick to apply forgiveness; deep love for Christ
Because of regeneration, *I have been made brand new, complete in Christ. I no longer need to experience the pain of shame.*	Christ-centered self-confidence; joy, courage, peace; desire to know Christ

Eleven

The Holy Spirit:
Our Source of Change

The truths we have examined in this book can have tremendous implications on our every goal and relationship, but now we need to understand how to actually implement them in our lives. How can we begin to experience positive change? Jesus answered this question in His last time of intimate instruction with His disciples (John 13-16). He told them that He would soon be put to death, but that they would not be left alone: *And I will ask the Father, and He will give you another Helper, that He may be with you forever* (John 14:16). That Helper is the Holy Spirit, who came some fifty days later to direct and empower the believers at Pentecost. That same Holy Spirit indwells each believer today, and serves as our instructor, counselor, and source of spiritual power as we live for Christ's glory and honor.

Who is the Holy Spirit, and why did He come? The Holy Spirit, the third Person of the Trinity, is God and possesses all the attributes of deity. His primary purpose is to glorify Christ and bring attention to Him. Christ said, *He shall glorify Me; for He shall take of Mine, and shall disclose it to you* (John 16:14). The Holy Spirit is our teacher, and He guides us into the truth of the Scriptures (John 16:13). It is by His power that the love of Christ flows through us and produces spiritual fruit within us (John 7:37-39; 15:1-8). This spiritual fruit is described in many ways in the New

Testament, including: intimate friendship with Christ (John 15:14); love for one another (John 15:12); joy and peace in the midst of difficulties (John 14:27; 15:11); steadfastness (Eph. 5:18-21); and evangelism and discipleship (Matt. 28:18-20).

Obviously, this fruit is not always evident in the lives of Christians, but why not?

As we all know, the Christian life is not an easy one. It is not simply a self-improvement program. True, we may at times be able to make some changes in our habits through our own discipline and determination, but Christianity is not merely self-effort. The Christian life is a supernatural one in which we draw on Christ as our resource for direction, encouragement, and strength. In one of the most widely-known metaphors of the Bible, Christ described the Christian life in John 15, using the illustration of a branch and a vine. He said:

> *I am the true vine, and My Father is the vine dresser.*
> *... Abide in* (live, grow, and gain your sustenance from) *Me, and I in you. As the branch cannot bear fruit of itself, unless it abides in the vine, so neither can you, unless you abide in Me.*
> *I am the vine, you are the branches; he who abides in Me, and I in him, he bears much fruit; for apart from Me you can do nothing.*
>
> John 15:1, 4-5

Nothing? Yes, in terms of that which honors Christ, is spiritually nourishing to us, and is genuine Christian service, anything done apart from the love and power of Christ amounts to nothing. Although we may expend tremendous effort at a great personal cost, only that which is done for Christ's glory in the power of His Spirit is of eternal value.

The very power of God that was evident when Christ was raised from the dead (Eph. 1:19-21) is available to every believer who abides in Him, who desires that He be honored, and who trusts that His Spirit will produce fruit in his or her life.

Just as the cross of Christ is the basis of our relationship with God, it is also the foundation of our spiritual growth. Christ's death is the supreme demonstration of God's love, power, and wisdom. The more we understand and apply the truths of justification, propitiation, reconciliation, and regeneration, the more our lives will reflect His character. Spiritual growth is not magic. It comes as we apply the love and forgiveness of Christ in our daily circumstances—reflecting on the unconditional acceptance of Christ and His awesome power, and choosing to respond to situations and people in light of His sovereign purpose and kindness toward us. As noted in the previous chapter, the Apostle Peter stated very clearly that our forgiveness, bought by the death of Christ, is the foundation of spiritual growth:

> *Now for this very reason also, applying all diligence, in your faith supply moral excellence, and in your moral excellence, knowledge;*
>
> *and in your knowledge, self-control, and in your self-control, perseverance, and in your perseverance, godliness;*
>
> *and in your godliness, brotherly kindness, and in your brotherly kindness, love.*
>
> *For if these qualities are yours and are increasing, they render you neither useless nor unfruitful in the true knowledge of our Lord Jesus Christ.*
>
> *For he who lacks these qualities is blind or shortsighted, having forgotten his purification from his former sins.*
>
> 2 Pet. 1:5-9

Again, the clear implication from this passage is that the absence of spiritual growth signifies one's lack of understanding concerning forgiveness. Seeking an emotional experience, going to seminar after seminar, or looking for a "deeper life" may not be the solution. Emotional experiences, seminars, and studies are only valid if they are founded on the love, forgiveness, and power of the cross and resurrection of Christ.

There is nothing more motivating, nothing more comforting, nothing else that compels us more to honor Christ, and nothing else that gives us as much compassion for others as the sacrificial payment of Christ which has rescued us from eternal condemnation.

At least five obstacles stem from a misunderstanding of Christ's love and forgiveness, and often prevent us from experiencing His presence and power:

1. We have wrong motives.
2. Our approach to the Christian life is too mechanical, or regimented.
3. We are too "mystical."
4. We lack knowledge about the availability of Christ's love and power.
5. We are harboring sin which blocks our fellowship with Christ.

Let's take a closer look at these obstacles:

Wrong Motives

Determining where we err in our motivations is often difficult. We usually have a variety of motives for what we pursue, and probably do nothing with completely pure motives. However, we must examine some of the reasons we may be following Christ before we can consider whether or not our motivations might be hindering our walk with Him.

Many of us tend to approach Christian living as a self-improvement program. We may desire spiritual growth, or we may have one or more fairly serious problems from which we desperately want to be delivered. While there is certainly nothing wrong with spiritual growth or desiring to be rid of a besetting problem, what is our motivation in wanting to achieve goals like these? Perhaps we desire success or the approval of others. Perhaps we fear that God can't really accept us until we have spiritually matured, or until "our problem" is removed. Perhaps we just want to feel better without having to struggle through the process of making major changes in our attitudes and behavior.

Motivations such as these may be mixed with a genuine desire to honor the Lord, but it's also possible that deep within us is a primary desire to glorify ourselves. When self-improvement becomes the center of our focus, rather than Christ, our focus is displaced.

It is important to understand that fruitfulness and growth are the *results* of focusing on Christ and desiring to honor Him. When growth and change are our primary goals, we tend to be preoccupied with ourselves instead of with Christ. *Am I growing? Am I getting any better? Am I more like Christ today? What am I learning?*

This inordinate preoccupation with self-improvement parallels our culture's self-help and personal enhancement movement in many ways. Personal development is certainly not wrong, but it is misleading—and it can be very disappointing—to make it our preeminent goal. If it is our goal at all, it should be secondary. As we grasp the unconditional love, grace, and power of God, then honoring Christ will increasingly be our consuming passion. God wants us to have a healthy self-awareness and to periodically analyze our lives, but He does not want us to be preoccupied with ourselves. The only One worthy of our preoccupation is Christ, our sovereign Lord, who told the Apostle Paul, *My grace is sufficient for you, for power is perfected in weakness* (2 Cor. 12:9).

If, through affirming Christian relationships, the power of God's Word, His Spirit, and time, we can begin to realize that our needs for security and approval are fully met in Christ, we will gradually be able to take our attention and affections off of ourselves, and place them on Him. Only then can we begin to adopt Paul's intense desire to honor Christ: *Therefore also we have as our ambition…to be pleasing to Him* (2 Cor. 5:9).

Too Mechanical

Some of us are too mechanical in our approach to the Christian life. Although we may rigorously schedule and discipline our lives in an effort to conform to what we believe is a biblical lifestyle, our lives may exhibit little of the freshness, joy, and spontaneity of Christ.

One man had organized his life into hourly segments, each designated to accomplish some particular "biblical purpose." True, he was organized and accomplished some good things, but he was miserable. This man was trusting in himself, instead of the Holy Spirit, to produce a life that pleased God.

Eventually, this man joined a church Bible study on God's grace. One of the men leading the group began meeting with him regularly. He had a lot of questions, and slowly, he began to realize that Christ's foremost commandment is to love Him and others (Matt. 22:36-40), and that joy, peace, and kindness are much more important to God than adhering to strict rules (for which Jesus rebuked the Pharisees). Over the next few months, as he continued in this affirming relationship, he gained a new perspective which later resulted in a new lifestyle of love and joy. This man is still an organized person, but being organized no longer dominates his life.

Though we may not be as extreme, many of us do have certain Christian activities (church attendance, tithing, Bible studies, etc.) that we feel we *must* do to be "good Christians." These activities themselves are obviously not wrong, but a performance-oriented perspective is wrong. Christ wants us to receive our joy and acceptance from Him instead of merely following rules or schedules. He is the Lord; He alone is our source of security, joy, and meaning.

Too Mystical

A third obstacle to abiding in Christ is becoming too *mystical*, or depending on supernatural feelings to dictate our relationship with God. This dependence on feelings leads to two problems. The first occurs when we wait for feelings to motivate us, and the other occurs when we see virtually every emotion as a "sign" from God. Let's examine these:

Some of us won't get up in the morning until the Lord "tells us to." We may not want to share Christ with others until we feel that God is prompting us. What we may be forgetting is that Christianity is primarily faith in action. Our emotions are not the most reliable source of motivation. Yes, the Holy Spirit does sometimes prompt us through impressions, but He has already given us the vast majority of what He wants us to do through the Scriptures. Rather than waiting for a "holy zap" to get us going, we need to believe the truth of God's Word and take action for His glory. Must we wait until we *feel* like loving other Christians, praying, studying the Scriptures, sharing our faith, or serving His cause? No. We need to follow the examples recounted in Hebrews 11 of the men and women who acted on their faith in God, often in spite of their feelings. True, these people were often reflective, and prayed for God's direction, but they always acted on His truth.

The second problem with depending on our feelings occurs when we believe that our emotions are a primary means of God's communication with us and are, therefore, signs from God which indicate His leading. This conclusion may compel us to make authoritative statements about God's will (for both ourselves and others) that are based on little more than how we feel. As in the first extreme, the Scriptures may take a back seat as we sometimes justify foolish and even immoral acts by this false "leading from the Lord."

Though the Scriptures encourage us to be real and honest about our emotions, they never tell us to live by them. Biblical truths are the only reliable guide for our lives. Our feelings may reinforce these truths, but they may also reflect Satan's lies that God doesn't love us, that the fun of a particular sin is more satisfying than following God, or that God will never answer our prayers. The truth of God's Word is our authority, not our feelings.

Does this mean that we should repress our feelings or deny that we have them? No, but we need a safe environment (a friend or small group) with whom we can be honest about how we feel. We also should express our feelings to the Lord, fully and freely, and look at the Scriptures to determine what He would have us do. Then, with the encouragement of mature believers, the power of His Spirit, and in obedience to His Word, we should do what honors Christ. Many times, when we obey Christ in spite of our feelings, the emotions of joy and peace will follow sooner or later.

Again, our emotions are God-given; it is not wrong to have them, but by themselves, our feelings aren't enough to determine God's direction in our lives. Understanding God's leading requires that we blend a proper understanding of the Scriptures with a sensitivity to His Spirit. The Bible is our ultimate authority, and we need to become good students of it so that we will understand both the character and will of God. As Paul told Timothy:

> *All Scripture is inspired by God and profitable for teaching,*
> *for reproof, for correction, for training in righteousness,*
> *that the man of God may be adequate, equipped for every*
> *good work.*
>
> 2 Tim. 3:16-17

We also need to develop a sensitivity to the Holy Spirit's leading that goes beyond emotionalism. This sensitivity takes time to develop, and is an awareness of His conviction of sin, what He wants us to say and do in certain situations, His prompting to share the gospel, etc. Discerning whether or not an impression is of God comes from three primary sources: the clear teaching of the Scriptures, previous experiences of learning, and the agreement of mature believers. If an impression is from God, it will not violate biblical principles.

Lack of Knowledge

Many of us are hindered in our walk with God because we do not realize the nature and depth of the love and power available to us in Christ.

132

We haven't yet fully comprehended the magnificent truths of the Scriptures—*that we are deeply loved, totally forgiven, fully pleasing, totally accepted, and complete in Christ,* with all the power of His resurrection available to us. We may be like the West Texas sheep rancher who lived in poverty even though vast resources of oil were under his property. He was fabulously rich but didn't even know it. Since its discovery many years ago, the Yates oil field has proven to be one of the richest and most productive in the world. Similarly, we have incredible resources available to us through the Holy Spirit, who enables us to experience the reality of Christ's love and power in many ways, including:

- Expressing Christ-like characteristics to us through other believers over a period of time (John 13:34-35; 1 John 4:7, 12).
- Revealing sin in our lives so that we can confess it and prevent our fellowship with God from being hindered (1 John 1:9).
- Helping us choose to honor Christ in our circumstances and relationships (2 Cor. 5:9).
- Enabling us to endure as we follow Christ (Rom. 5:1-5).
- Producing spiritual fruit in our lives (John 15:1-8; Gal. 5:22-23).

Harboring Sin

Willful sin is a fifth obstacle that clouds our fellowship with God. Indeed, sin may be pleasurable for a moment, but inevitably, its destructive nature will reveal itself in many ways: broken relationships, poor self-esteem, and a poor witness for Christ. Whether it is a blatant sin of immorality or the more subtle sin of pride, we must learn to deal with all sin decisively, for our benefit and for Christ's glory.

Christ's death paid for all of our sins; they are completely forgiven. Comprehending His love and forgiveness encourages us to admit that we have sinned and claim forgiveness for any and every sin as soon as we become aware of it. Again, this prevents our fellowship with Christ from being hindered, and enables us to continue experiencing His love and power.

Paul wrote to the Galatian Christians:

> *...The fruit of the Spirit is love, joy, peace, patience,*
> *kindness, goodness, faithfulness,*
> *gentleness, self-control. . . .*
>
> Gal. 5:22-23

As we respond to the love of Christ and trust His Spirit to fill us, these characteristics will become increasingly evident in our lives. The filling of the Holy Spirit includes two major aspects: our purpose (to bring honor to Christ instead of to ourselves) and our resources (trusting in His love and power to accomplish results, instead of trusting in our own wisdom and abilities). Although we will continue to mature in our relationship with the Lord over the years, we can begin to experience His love, strength, and purpose from the moment we put Him at the center of our lives.

Spencer, a junior at the University of Missouri, had been a Christian for several years. He had trusted Christ as his personal Savior when a friend from his dorm shared the gospel with him during his first semester. Although he was growing in his relationship with Christ, intramural athletics and parties with his rowdy friends became the focus of Spencer's life by the middle of his sophomore year. He still went to church frequently, but he was confused and often felt guilty about his relationships with his friends and their activities. He tried talking with them about this, but they only laughed. Despite his occasional feelings of discomfort, Spencer felt like he needed these friends, and he continued spending time with them.

Then, in the fall of his junior year, Spencer went to several Christian meetings on campus. He began hearing about the love and power of Christ, and how the Holy Spirit can enable us to live for Him.

Another young man, Phil, took an interest in Spencer, and began to disciple him. Through Phil's supportive friendship, Spencer began to develop an eternal perspective, slowly recognizing that worldliness and sin are destructive, but that following Christ is eternally significant. One night, Spencer spent some time alone, praying and thinking about what he had learned. He realized that his life was confusing, frustrating, and dishonoring to the Lord. Spencer also realized that Christ is worthy of his love and obedience, and decided to live for Him. As he began to confess the specific sins the Holy Spirit brought to his mind, and as he asked Him for the power to live in a way that is pleasing to Christ, Spencer felt a surge of relief and joy. He was doing the right thing.

Phil was excited about the steps Spencer was taking, but Spencer was primarily concerned about his other friends. Realizing that he might be rejected, Spencer made plans to tell them about his decision to follow Christ. When he did, some of them laughed. Others were surprised, and a few were even angry. For the next year, Spencer still spent some time with these friends, but now at ball games instead of wild parties. He shared Christ with many of them, and had the joy of seeing two trust Christ. Spencer had plenty of struggles and spiritual growing pains, but his life began to reflect a new consistency, a new purpose, and a new attitude of thankfulness to the Lord.

Like Spencer, our own willingness to be filled with the Holy Spirit is a direct response to the magnificent truths centered in the cross and resurrection of Christ, and our participation in relationships in which we sense His love for us. *We are deeply loved and completely forgiven by God, fully pleasing to God, totally accepted by God, and complete in Him.*

Are you depending on God's Spirit to teach you, change you, and use you in the lives of others? If so, continue trusting Him! If not, review the five obstacles to following Christ and see if any of these are obstructing your relationship with Him. Are there specific sins you need to confess? *Confession* means to agree with God that you have sinned and that Christ has completely forgiven you. It also means "to repent," to turn from your sins to a life of love and obedience to God.

As you continue in the process of experiencing more of God's grace, take time to reflect on His love and power. Trust Him to guide you by His Word, fill you with His Spirit, and enable you to live for Him and be used by Him in the lives of others. Abiding in Christ does not mean deliverance from all of your problems, but it will provide a powerful relationship with the One who is the source of wisdom for difficult decisions, love to encourage you, and strength to help you endure.

Twelve

Renewing the Mind

In one of the most famous dialogues in the Bible, Jesus explained the profound truth of regeneration to Nicodemus:

> ...*unless one is born again, he cannot see the kingdom of God....*
>
> *That which is born of the flesh is flesh, and that which is born of the Spirit is spirit.*
>
> *Do not marvel that I said to you, "You must be born again."*
>
> John 3:3, 6-7

When we were born, we entered a world ruled by Satan, and we learned the ways of the world. *You are of your father the devil,* Jesus explained, *and you want to do the desires of your father* (John 8:44). Words like these make it easy for us to understand why we believe Satan's lies so readily!

However, at some point in our lives, the Holy Spirit drew us to Christ, and we trusted Him to forgive us and give us new purpose and meaning in our existence. The Holy Spirit baptized us into the body of Christ, a new spiritual family, the family of God. He plucked us from the family of Satan (Col. 1:13-14) and adopted us into God's eternal family as sons and daughters (Rom. 8:15). We were cursed to die as members of Satan's family, but as members of God's family, we were granted everything pertaining to life and godliness at the very moment of our new birth. We were not forced to qualify to receive God's provisions, but instead have received the rights and privileges of sons by His grace and mercy.

If an earthly father receives his newborn son into his arms and gives the child good things, how much more does our heavenly Father give to His children? When we are born into an earthly family, we are given a name, all the provisions of food, clothing, and shelter to sustain us, and perhaps we are even made the beneficiary of a savings account for our future. All of the father's abilities to provide for his child start to work on the child's behalf before he or she even begins to perform. Children are bound to their earthly fathers by the unconditional right of birth, not by their ability to perform.

How much more are newly-born children of God bound to their heavenly Father! As His children, we are endowed with the Holy Spirit to lead and convict us, and are given all the capability needed to honor God and live purposeful and meaningful lives. All of His provisions become ours at our spiritual birth, before we do good or evil.

And yet, as babes in Christ, we need to grow in our understanding and experience of Christ's life in us. We may rebel, but God is long-suffering and willing to give us loving correction and instruction. We may fail Him, but we are still His children.

It is interesting that when the Holy Spirit gave us a new spirit, He did not give us a totally renewed mind. Although the Spirit of Christ lives within us and enables us to evaluate our experiences, our minds tend to dwell on the worldly thoughts of our old nature instead of on God's truth. We are in conflict, torn between our new godly motivation to glorify Christ and our old motivations of lust and pride. Paul recognized this conflict. He wrote the Christians in Rome:

I find then the principle that evil is present in me, the one who wishes to do good.

For I joyfully concur with the law of God in the inner man,

but I see a different law in the members of my body, waging war against the law of my mind, and making me a prisoner of the law of sin which is in my members.

Wretched man that I am! Who will set me free from the body of this death?

Thanks be to God through Jesus Christ our Lord!...

Rom. 7:21-25

How then can we break free from the law of sin and begin to grow in Christ? How can we assist in the process that will enable us to follow Him?

To change our behavior, we usually need to see others who are being honest, and who are in the process of applying spiritual truths to their lives. In this environment, and through our personal study of God's Word, we can reject earthly thoughts and replace them with those that are spiritual. Solomon wrote, *As [a man] thinks within himself, so he is* (Prov. 23:7). Our thoughts usually affect the way we feel, the way we perceive ourselves and others, and ultimately, the way we act. The way we think can determine whether we will live according to God's truth or the world's value system. Still writing to the Christians in Rome, Paul explained the serious implications of how we think:

And do not be conformed to this world, but be transformed by the renewing of your mind, that you may prove what the will of God is, that which is good and acceptable and perfect.

Rom. 12:2

Although the way we think often affects the way we feel (and thus, the way we act), it is also true that feelings affect our thoughts and behavior, and that our behavior can affect our feelings and our thinking. In the verse preceding the one we just examined, Paul wrote, *I urge you therefore, brethren, by the mercies of God* (an appeal to their feelings about God's grace toward them) *to present your bodies a living and holy sacrifice, acceptable to God. . . .* This relationship of thinking, feeling, and acting is not always unidirectional. Our thoughts, emotions, and behaviors are dependent on each other; none exists in a vacuum. Changing how we think, feel, and act is a process that involves the supernatural work of the Holy Spirit, honesty, time, modeling, affirmation, and truth. As a starting point, however, we will use a model adapted from psychologist Albert Ellis's Rational Emotive Therapy. A simple explanation of this approach is:

Situations

⇩

Beliefs ⇨ Thoughts ⇨ Emotions ⇨ Actions

We often interpret the situations we encounter through our beliefs. Some of our interpretations are conscious reflections; most of them, however, are based on unconscious assumptions. These beliefs trigger certain thoughts, which, in turn, stimulate certain emotions, and from these emotions come our actions. In order for an emotion to persist, our belief system must continue to produce certain thoughts. For example, we often will not stay sad without continuing to think sad thoughts. Think of it in this way: Our minds contain deeply held beliefs and attitudes which have been learned through our environment, experiences, and education. These beliefs and attitudes produce thoughts which reflect how we perceive the events in our lives. These thoughts, then, combined with past experiences, relationships, and patterns of behavior, are often the source of our emotions, and our emotions are usually the launching pad for our actions.

Understanding ourselves and how we think can help us in two ways: we can learn how to manage our responses to current events, and we can learn how to experience healing from the damage of our past. Understanding that our thoughts are usually products of our beliefs gives us a tool for exposing those beliefs and identifying their source. Which false belief do the following thoughts expose?

- *He just has to like me.*
- *What can I do to make her like me more?*
- *I'm afraid he's given up on me.*

All of these thoughts reveal a belief in Satan's lie that we must be approved by certain people to have self-worth. In this same manner, many of our thoughts can be traced back to our beliefs—beliefs which are either founded on the truths of Scripture, or the lies of Satan.

False beliefs may be based on a partially accurate perception of circumstances. For example, it may be accurate that you failed to get a report in on time. You did actually fail, but that is only part of the truth. The other part is that your self-worth is not affected by that failure. To recognize your failure, but then believe that your failure has caused you to lose self-worth, is to believe both a truth and a lie. The facts may be true, but our interpretation of those facts may be based on the crafty deceit of Satan.

Sometimes, a completely accurate perception may trigger a whole array of emotions and unconscious thoughts, some of which are accurate, and some of which stem from false beliefs. For example, Kay's accurate perception, *My husband is drinking again,* actually represents many of the following unconscious thoughts:

- *I hate that inconsiderate bum!*
- *He'll start mistreating the children and me.*
- *I'll finally have to move out.*
- *I'll be forced to provide for the children and myself.*
- *I don't have any skills that qualify me to earn a living.*
- *I'm nothing but a failure.*
- *My friends won't have anything to do with me.*
- *Maybe God is punishing me.*

Kay was responding emotionally, not only to the conscious thought of her husband's drinking, but to her unconscious fears as well. The combination of her accurate perceptions and speculative assumptions formed a mental framework which spawned her emotions, and eventually, her actions.

We need to analyze our thoughts in each circumstance to determine which are valid and which are not.

I recall dealing with an ongoing sense of personal failure on several occasions when I experienced rejection. In one instance particularly, I felt consumed by feelings of hurt, anger, self-pity, and depression. I prayed about the situation as often as I could bring myself to face it; I read portions of the Scriptures at length, and several weeks after the relationship had ended, I talked with an objective friend about it.

Through this process, I gradually realized that my negative feelings were not only based on the pain of having been rejected by someone I cared for, but on the *implications* of that person's rejection. The implications, or false beliefs, I later identified were: *I will never have another relationship like the one that just ended. I will never be able to get over the pain this relationship has caused me. I'm just not any good at interpersonal relationships, and I never will be. I am obviously inferior because this person, whom I valued, has rejected me.*

Only as I began to realize that my emotions were largely the product of false beliefs—many of which stemmed from some misperceptions I had about myself during childhood—did I begin to recover from the injury of having been rejected. Granted, I still had to deal with painful feelings of loss caused by the ending of this relationship. But realizing that my negative emotions were primarily caused by my false beliefs—rather than the event itself—was enormously liberating for me.

For many of us, the majority of our beliefs were formed before we became Christians; therefore, it is easy to understand why many of our actions do not reflect Christ's character. Until those false beliefs are identified, ruthlessly rooted out, and replaced with biblical convictions, our lives will continue to be filled with destructive thoughts and actions.

Because of our fallen human nature, all of us experience false beliefs which contradict God's Word. Failure to recognize them can have devastating effects on our lives.

For example, a young girl named Dawn was sent to me by her parents, who hoped I could reason with her about her promiscuous behavior. But Dawn could not understand how something that felt so good and made her so happy could be wrong.

Over the course of several weeks, Dawn began to discuss her circumstances more openly with me. She explained that her father spent so much time working that he had little time for her and her mother. Dawn had been neglected, and after several meetings together, her wall of defenses eroded and she cried, "I just want to be loved, that's all!" Her behavior had been her unconscious attempt to feel close to someone. She had enjoyed it primarily because she finally felt loved, even though most of these men were really using her and not loving her at all.

Dawn eventually joined a support group, where she met other young women who were learning about the pain of their past and their hope for the future. These women could identify with Dawn's dreams and fears. They encouraged her and each other to gain a new sense of identity based on their love for each other and the truth of God's Word. This process hasn't been easy for Dawn, but her progress is real.

The case of Winston also provides a clear example of how we can experience progress in our circumstances by identifying our false beliefs. Winston was an older man with only a few years left until retirement. But he had become particularly anxious since he had gotten a new boss who was giving him degrading tasks seemingly designed to run him off. The pressure upset Winston so much that he was seriously considering an early retirement. When he came to me for advice and explained the situation, he was surprised when I told him that his problem wasn't his new boss, but the way he was perceiving the situation.

"What!" exclaimed Winston. "Are you trying to tell me that the awful way I'm being treated isn't really what's making me feel depressed?"

"Yes," I said. "Your anxiety comes from your perception of yourself and your job."

I explained to Winston that he was operating by the false belief that he must be approved by his boss in order to be happy. I also suggested that God was possibly allowing him to experience this situation so that he could begin learning how to be less dependent on the approval of others and more dependent on God. This would eventually enable him to count on what really matters in life: *that he is deeply loved by God, completely forgiven, fully pleasing, totally accepted, and complete in Christ,* resulting in a life of love and depth and meaning.

For the next several weeks, we talked about his anger toward his supervisor and the hurt he felt at the thought of being replaced. As Winston was honest about his emotions, he was better able to perceive God's unconditional love for him. He got involved in a prayer group at his church where he experienced the understanding and encouragement of others.

Several months later, I saw Winston again. He told me, "I still feel the sting of my boss's harassment, but at least I now have some friends who understand me. Their encouragement to be honest about my feelings has allowed me to experience more of God's love."

One of the greatest characteristics of personal maturity in Christ is the ability to be honest about how we really feel about a person or situation, and the willingness to accept full responsibility for our emotional and behavioral reactions in the disturbing circumstances of life. In realizing that our circumstances aren't the cause of our self-destructive reactions, and by applying God's truths to those situations, we can gain peace and perspective.

The world need not have control over us. Our spiritual battles may be intense, but we will be able to persevere if we can begin to analyze our circumstances through God's perspective and reject the false beliefs which often control our emotions and actions. Faith in God's Word prevents us from being buffeted by difficult situations, or having to live "under the circumstances." In Phil. 4: 8-9, Paul admonished the Christians in Philippi to focus their attention on truth:

Finally, brethren, whatever is true, whatever is honorable, whatever is right, whatever is pure, whatever is lovely, whatever is of good repute, if there is any excellence and if anything worthy of praise, let your mind dwell on these things.

The things you have learned and received and heard and seen in me, practice these things; and the God of peace shall be with you.

Identifying our false beliefs is the first step on our path toward new freedom in Jesus Christ. Once we recognize that many of our deeply-held beliefs are actually rooted in deception, we can begin using our emotions as a checkpoint to determine if we are basing our beliefs about a given circumstance on the truth or lies. Many of our painful emotions, such as fear, anger, and tension, are often the product of believing Satan's lies. Therefore, when we experience these emotions, we can ask ourselves, *What am I believing in this situation?* In almost every case, we will be able to trace our negative emotions back to one of Satan's false beliefs. We can then choose to reject the lie we have identified and replace it with the corresponding truth from the Scriptures. This process is amazingly simple, yet profound and applicable. Don's situation offers a good example:

Don was working hard on a mortgage loan proposal when his boss walked in to check on his progress. James, another man in the office who wanted a promotion very badly, made a joke about all the papers scattered on Don's desk. Their boss had a good laugh, and they walked out together.

Don was furious! He had worked diligently on that proposal, and it was excellent, yet James had made fun of him in front of his boss. But instead of fuming about the incident all day, Don used his anger as a gauge for his beliefs. He stopped and asked himself, *Why am I responding this way? What am I believing?* After a few minutes, he identified two false beliefs: *I must be approved by certain others to feel good about myself,* and *those who fail* (James and his boss had failed to treat Don the way he wanted to be treated) *are unworthy of love and deserve to be condemned.*

145

Don was honest about his anger, and determined to reject Satan's lies and focus on the truths that he is totally accepted by God and that he can love others with Christ's love. Though he was still unhappy about the incident, he felt encouraged that he was able to be honest about his emotions and apply God's Word to his thoughts and circumstances.

In examining our emotions, it is important to realize that not all distressing emotions reflect deception. For example, the emotion of remorse might be the Holy Spirit's conviction leading us to repentance. Anger with someone for molesting a child or beating an elderly person is righteous anger, just as a measure of fear while driving during rush hour is entirely justifiable!

In our problem-filled world, there are at least two ways that many of us choose to deal with our emotions and surrounding circumstances. One is to shut them out completely, refusing to acknowledge their presence or to be affected by them; the other is to become enslaved to them.

Switching off our emotions can cause us to become callous and insensitive to ourselves and those around us. Unfortunately, this is just what happened to Mike.

Over the years, Mike had deadened himself to his emotions, apparently not allowing anything to bother him. He had experienced a difficult childhood, first being abandoned by his parents, and then being shuffled from one relative to another. In an effort to stop the pain, Mike learned to block out his feelings and to ignore his circumstances.

Mike's success at suppressing his emotions had long-lasting consequences. First, by severing himself from his painful feelings, he missed out on many pleasant ones as well. Secondly, the longer Mike avoided dealing with his emotions, the more fearful he became of them. To combat this fear, he simply became more calloused and withdrawn. Third, and perhaps most importantly, Mike could not use his emotions to detect the false beliefs that were at the root of his problems, because he denied that he even had those emotions. He was helpless, unable to acknowledge his needs.

Melinda, on the other hand, wore her emotions on her sleeve. She wasn't difficult to figure out. Her flaring temper, her torrent of tears, and her jovial laughter were all indications of her rollercoaster emotions. Never knowing what to expect, Melinda's husband, Ken, became weary of trying to deal with his volatile wife.

Melinda's erratic mood swings affected her so much that they became, in effect, her lord. Her feelings seemed to be more real than anything else in her life and they clouded her perception of God and His purposes.

We often respond incorrectly to them, but our emotions are in fact a gift from God, intended to be used and enjoyed. Emotions are signals which tell us something about our environment. They can protect us by helping us to choose appropriate behavior. We can help ourselves (and others) by encouraging honesty and by allowing ourselves to fully experience both our positive and negative feelings. Emotions help us to determine what is really going on inside. In the same way that good parents allow their children to express hurt, and experience comfort and healing when they have fallen, we can do this for ourselves and others by advocating an honest expression of emotions and by applying comfort to the hurts each of us experience. In this way, we can avoid repression and denial, and encourage an appropriate expression of our emotions—within ourselves, with others, and with God.

The inability to experience and express feelings is as dangerous to our well-being as the inability to feel physical pain. As we become aware of painful emotions and destructive behavior, we need to acknowledge these feelings and actions to God in prayer, asking Him to reveal any false beliefs that may be hindering our fellowship with Him. Then, empowered by the Holy Spirit, and encouraged by the love and affirmation of others, we can learn to cast aside our false beliefs and choose to believe the truths of God's Word.

It is necessary to first expose our root emotions and the false beliefs which are triggering them. Then, by faith, we can allow God's Word to renew our minds.

Listed below are ten typical statements which reflect common false beliefs. Each is a reflection of the four false beliefs we have already studied:

1. *I must meet certain standards to feel good about myself.*
2. *I must be approved by certain others to feel good about myself.*
3. *Those who fail (including myself) are unworthy of love and deserve to be blamed and condemned.*
4. *I am what I am; I cannot change; I am hopeless.*

Examine each of these statements given below, asking, *What false belief(s) does this statement represent?* Then, beside each statement, place the number of one or more of the false beliefs:

1. *Tammy is right. I'll never be a successful husband and father.*_____
2. *I'm so undisciplined; I'll never be able to accomplish anything.*_____
3. *I just can't trust God.*_____
4. *My father never did accept me.*_____
5. *That's just the way I am.*_____
6. *Everything I do turns out badly.*_____
7. *I failed my college final. I'll never graduate now.*_____
8. *I can't overcome a particular sin.*_____
9. *I am going to fail financially.*_____
10. *I deserve all the misery I am experiencing.*_____

Compare your answers with these:

1.	1, 4	6.	1
2.	1, 4	7.	1, 3
3.	4	8.	4
4.	2	9.	1
5.	4	10.	3

Were you able to identify the false beliefs? If not, look at the statements again carefully, analyzing the root issue behind each one.

Sometimes, we tend to respond poorly to trying circumstances because we think we deserve better. Our society and media tell us that everybody should be happy, comfortable, healthy, and successful. The difficulty arises when we believe these statements, and equate orthodox Christianity with a comfortable, middle-class lifestyle. We think we deserve the best of everything, so when things don't go the way we'd like, we get upset.

What do you think you deserve? Appreciation from your friends, success in school or in your career, a clear complexion, good health, a promotion, leisure time, or freedom from whining children, an insensitive spouse, or inconsiderate neighbors? We sometimes are unable to identify the particular status or comfort we think we deserve, but are sure that we deserve better than what we're experiencing. One of the most obvious results of this perspective is a lack of thankfulness and contentment.

There are three principles from the Scriptures that can significantly help us understand what we deserve:

The Transcendent Purposes of God
The prophet Isaiah wrote that God's wisdom and purposes far surpass our own:

"For My thoughts are not your thoughts, neither are your ways My ways" declares the Lord.

"For as the heavens are higher than the earth, so are My ways higher than your ways, and My thoughts than your thoughts."

Is. 55:8-9

One reason we may think we deserve better is that we believe we know what is best for ourselves and for others. But we are not omniscient. We are not sovereign, gracious, and good like God. Do we really deserve better than what the sovereign, Almighty God has for us?

A Humble View of Ourselves

Christ told a parable to explain our proper relationship to God:

But which of you, having a slave plowing or tending sheep, will say to him when he has come in from the field, "Come immediately and sit down to eat"?

But will he not say to him, "Prepare something for me to eat, and properly clothe yourself and serve me until I have eaten and drunk; and afterward you will eat and drink"?

He does not thank the slave because he did the things which were commanded, does he?

So you too, when you do all the things which are commanded you, say, "We are unworthy slaves; we have done only that which we ought to have done."

Luke 17:7-10

Jesus is the Lord. He is the One who rightly deserves our affection and joyful obedience. Jesus said of the servant in this passage that if he did all that he was commanded, he was still to think of himself as an unworthy servant. *Unworthy? I thought we were deeply loved and accepted by God.* This passage does not contradict the biblical truths we have examined. It teaches a different issue than the basis of acceptance before God: that He is the sovereign Lord, and does not owe us anything. All that we have is by His grace. We are the thankful recipients; He is the gracious and loving Lord.

The problem with feeling deserving usually appears when we do something for the Lord: Bible study, church attendance, witnessing, or being kind to someone, and then think that He is obligated to bless us. God is never obligated to bless us, but does what is best for His honor and our growth.

Overwhelming Thankfulness for Our Forgiveness

In Luke 7:36-50, a woman who is overcome with thankfulness for her forgiveness is contrasted with a Pharisee who is not thankful:

> *Now one of the Pharisees was requesting Him to dine with him. And He entered the Pharisee's house, and reclined at the table.*
>
> *And behold, there was a woman in the city who was a sinner; and when she learned that He was reclining at the table in the Pharisee's house, she brought an alabaster vial of perfume,*
>
> *and standing behind Him at His feet, weeping, she began to wet His feet with her tears, and kept wiping them with the hair of her head, and kissing His feet, and anointing them with the perfume.*
>
> *Now when the Pharisee who had invited Him saw this, he said to himself, "If this man were a prophet He would know who and what sort of person this woman is who is touching Him, that she is a sinner."*
>
> *And Jesus answered and said to him, "Simon, I have something to say to you." And he replied, "Say it, Teacher."*
>
> *"A certain moneylender had two debtors: one owed five hundred denarii and the other fifty. When they were unable to*

repay, he graciously forgave them both. Which of them therefore will love him more?"

Simon answered and said, "I suppose the one whom he forgave more." And He said to him, "You have judged correctly."

And turning toward the woman, He said to Simon, "Do you see this woman? I entered your house; you gave Me no water for My feet, but she has wet My feet with her tears, and wiped them with her hair.

"You gave Me no kiss; but she, since the time I came in, she has not ceased to kiss My feet.

"You did not anoint My head with oil, but she anointed My feet with perfume.

"For this reason I say to you, her sins, which are many, have been forgiven, for she loved much; but he who is forgiven little, loves little."

And He said to her, "Your sins have been forgiven."

And those who were reclining at the table with Him began to say to themselves, "Who is this man who even forgives sins?"

And He said to the woman, "Your faith has saved you; go in peace."

Does your response to Christ resemble that of the Pharisee or that of the woman? The more we are able to grasp even a portion of the magnitude of Christ's love and forgiveness, the more we will tend to overflow with appreciation to Him.

Some of the influences on our minds have been very positive; some have been harmful. For good or bad, our thoughts have been shaped by years of parental modeling, friendships, past experiences, choices we have made, our culture, the media, and many other factors. Our perceptions about God and about ourselves do not usually change by reading a verse or two of Scripture. Renewing our minds is a lifelong process. It is often painfully slow, but diligent study of God's Word, trust in the Holy Spirit's power to change us, and the encouragement of other believers can produce minds and lives that are healthy, honest, and fruitful for the kingdom of God.

Thirteen
The Weapons of Our Warfare

One of the biggest steps we can take toward consistently glorifying Christ and walking in peace and joy with our heavenly Father is to recognize the deceit which has held us captive. Satan's lies distort our true perspective, warp our thoughts, and produce painful emotions. If we cannot identify those lies, then it is very likely that we will continue to be defeated by them.

However, simply identifying the source of our problems will not free us from them. Once we recognize the tricks of the enemy, we must seize the offense. We must use the weapons God has provided to overcome incorrect thoughts, vain imaginations, and distorted beliefs. Paul describes the Christian's armor and weaponry this way:

> *Therefore, take up the full armor of God, that you may be able to resist in the evil day, and having done everything, to stand firm.*
> *Stand firm therefore, having girded your loins with truth, and having put on the breastplate of righteousness, and having shod your feet with the preparation of the gospel of peace;*

in addition to all, taking up the shield of faith with which you will be able to extinguish all the flaming missiles of the evil one.

And take the helmet of salvation, and the sword of the Spirit, which is the word of God.

Eph. 6:13-17

Paul instructs us to put on the *full* armor of God. This armor is defensive, able to protect us from the attacks of Satan. Paul goes on to encourage us to take up *the sword of the Spirit, which is the word of God.* In contrast to the defensive armor, God's Word is an offensive weapon, and is used to attack the enemy and conquer him. Paul indicates that Christ does not intend for Christians to sit idly in their armor and absorb attack after attack from Satan. Instead, the wise warrior will reach for his offensive weapon and destroy the enemy's fortresses. Applying this to our study, we need to take the truths of God's Word and use them to attack and overcome Satan's lies.

Paul explains the nature of our warfare:

For though we walk in the flesh, we do not war according to the flesh,

for the weapons of our warfare are not of the flesh, but divinely powerful for the destruction of fortresses.

We are destroying speculations and every lofty thing raised up against the knowledge of God, and we are taking every thought captive to the obedience of Christ.

2 Cor. 10:3-5

For many of us, our family backgrounds have been very painful. Alcoholism, drug abuse, divorce, workaholism, violence, or other family disorders have left us with deep emotional scars. We may feel neglected, lonely, angry, hurt, or numb. We may consequently believe that we are unlovable people who are unworthy of being cared for by others, and that

God is like our parents: harsh, condemning, manipulative, or aloof. These emotions and self-perceptions form a strong fortress that has been founded on Satan's lies and communicated to us by those who were supposed to love, protect, and provide for us. Concepts like these don't vanish quickly. Often, our first step toward progress is realizing that we have been hurting for a long time, but have refused to admit it, or perhaps, that our defense mechanisms of drivenness or withdrawal have been protecting us from the reality of our pain.

Through the process of being honest and experiencing comfort from the Lord and others, these fortresses can be slowly torn down. They are overcome by *destroying speculations and every lofty thing raised up against the knowledge of God;* that is, by identifying and rejecting specific lies, and then replacing them with the truth.

In the same letter to the Christians in Corinth, Paul shows how repentance can be a vital weapon in our warfare. If we have been deceived by the enemy, or if we have been involved in willful disobedience to God, we can repent by turning from our sin to God. Paul rejoiced that the Corinthians repented and experienced God's grace:

> *I now rejoice, not that you were made sorrowful, but that you were made sorrowful to the point of repentance; for you were made sorrowful according to the will of God, in order that you might not suffer loss in anything through us.*
>
> *For the sorrow that is according to the will of God produces a repentance without regret, leading to salvation; but the sorrow of the world produces death.*
>
> 2 Cor. 7:9-10

The Corinthians' example demonstrates repentance as a tactical weapon of our spiritual warfare. *Repentance* means "to change"; to change one's mind, purpose, and actions. It is more than just the experience of sorrow; it is the changing of our attitude and actions when we have realized that they are sinful and dishonoring to God.

As an offensive weapon, repentance has two sharp edges. The first allows us to discern and reject false beliefs. When situations occur which trigger certain beliefs that produce ungodly responses, we must:

1. Be honest about our emotions.
2. Trace the emotions back to their source and identify the false belief(s).
3. Consciously and assertively reject the false belief(s).

The following diagram illustrates this process:

Trace the emotions back to the false beliefs.

The second edge of repentance is the replacement of false beliefs with the truth of God's Word. By affirming God's truth about our worth, we will lodge it deep within our hearts and minds, and begin to reshape our thinking, feelings, and behavior. Then, the process of having the truth modeled to us, affirmed in us, taught to us, and applied by us over time will enable us to increasingly experience freedom in different areas of our lives.

If false beliefs remain in our minds, unchallenged and unrejected, they retain an unconscious influence on our emotions and reactions. Consequently, our warfare is a sustained and continuous battle. Every disturbing situation provides us with an opportunity to discover our incorrect thinking, to reject our world-acquired beliefs, and exchange them for the truth. This is a daily process for every Christian; only this aggressive, conscious, truth-seeking effort can reverse years of habitually wrong thinking.

Affirming God's truth is a weapon of great spiritual value. Through this process, we state God's truth as our own perspective. Continual affirmation gradually produces beliefs which result in correct thinking, which then result in godly responses. Affirming the truths of God's Word enables us to overcome the deception of the enemy (Rev. 12:10). The following diagram illustrates this process:

In practice, our actual experience may not be quite so neat and precise. Our emotions, beliefs, and behavior are the product of years of experiences and relationships. They can be very strong, very confusing, and very difficult to understand.

Although the above diagram is a general model, it is helpful in identifying some of the roots of our behavior and emotions, and can serve as an aid to direct us to follow God's truth in our growth process.

The circumstances of Stewart, a good friend of mine, may better illustrate how we can apply this double edge of repentance to our false belief system:

Stewart was raised in a dysfunctional family. His father, an alcoholic, was emotionally distant from his family, and disinterested in their concerns. His mother, in an effort to control her household, was manipulative and condemning. Nothing Stewart did as a child merited his father's interest or his mother's approval. The result was that Stewart felt unloved and incompetent. He responded by becoming a persistent people-pleaser, always hoping that by working a little harder, he would win his parents' approval and acceptance.

When Stewart became a Christian, he transferred his people-pleasing tendencies to his relationships with God and other believers. He joined a local church, and within a short time, became active in several of its ministry programs. Because he was responsible, conscientious, and sensitive to others, Stewart quickly became a valuable resource for assistance and advice. And he was happy to help. His role within the church gave him a special sense of significance and purpose. He felt highly esteemed by others and by God.

But as the years passed, Stewart's involvement with church activities became more demanding. Members were calling him at work and at home to attend meetings, lead studies, lend financial support, or more often, because they needed someone to listen. Wanting to gain approval from others, and striving to please God, Stewart dutifully complied to all of these demands and more. As a result, his output at work began to diminish. At home, his wife questioned whom he'd married: her or their church.

At first, Stewart reasoned that he was managing his time poorly, and compensated by cutting back on his sleep to get more done. But gradually, as the pressures around him increased, Stewart began to harbor feelings of resentment and anger toward members of his church. And, though he continued to adhere to his daily devotional schedule with God, he felt increasingly distant from Him. When his marriage became jeopardized and his boss confronted him with the possibility of losing his job, Stewart began to wonder if God really cared for him at all.

Feeling threatened and disillusioned, he finally sought the advice of a trusted friend. When this friend asked Stewart some pointed questions about his family background, he started taking an objective look at how he was raised for the first time. What he saw filled him with both pain and outrage.

In conversations with his parents over the next year, Stewart started recognizing that his hurt and anger were rooted in his fears of their rejection and perception of him as a failure. Through the help of his friend, he also began to notice patterns in his relationships with God and with others which indicated that he was basing his actions and self-worth on the beliefs that he must meet certain standards and be approved by certain others to feel good about himself.

When Stewart realized the degree to which he'd been affected by his family background, he was devastated and felt more incompetent than ever. Gradually, however, he began to understand that his new insights could be a driving force toward change in his life.

Over the next several years, as he identified false beliefs in his motivations to please and perform, he learned how to reject those beliefs and replace them with God's Word. Stewart's life slowly began to change. He started gaining a healthy sense of independence from his parents, and with it, self-respect. As a result, he began to assume responsibility for his own welfare. He resolved to put his wife and children first among his priorities, joined an athletic club, and began seeking supportive relationships. God has since used those relationships and others to convey His message of love for Stewart.

Today, Stewart is still active within his church, but he is more selective about the ways he involves himself there. Though he still desires to please others, and occasionally uses performance to measure his value, Stewart can now more easily recognize and reject false beliefs, and allow himself to feel affirmed by the truth of God's Word.

To effectively utilize affirmation as a weapon for change, remember these concepts:

• *Affirming the truths of the Scriptures does not mean that our natural mind will agree with what we are affirming.* The Bible teaches that the natural mind is antagonistic toward God:

> *But I say, walk by the Spirit, and you will not carry out the desire of the flesh.*
>
> *For the flesh sets its desire against the Spirit, and the Spirit against the flesh; for these are in opposition to one another, so that you may not do the things that you please.*
>
> Gal. 5:16-17

It may be uncomfortable to reflect on the truths of God's Word because they oppose the lies of the enemy. Don't be surprised by spiritual conflict when you confront these lies with God's truths.

• *Realize that we can't hope to achieve spiritual growth and change through self-effort.* The Holy Spirit is our Helper, and He will point out those circumstances in which we are believing Satan's lies; He will give us insight into the truth of the Scriptures; and He will give us strength to persevere in spiritual battle. Even our desire to honor Christ is due to the Holy Spirit's work in our lives. Through His wisdom and power, and through our moment-by-moment choice to follow Him, the Holy Spirit produces changes in our lives for the glory of Christ.

• *In order to become proficient at affirming these truths, we need to become students of God's Word, and allow its truth to lodge deep within our hearts and minds.* We should make it a regular practice to meditate upon the Scriptures so that the Holy Spirit can use them to change our beliefs, thoughts, emotions, and actions. David explained the power of applying God's Word:

> *Thy Word I have treasured in my heart, that I may not sin against Thee. . . .*
>
> *If Thy law had not been my delight, then I would have perished in my affliction. I will never forget Thy precepts, for by them Thou hast revived me.*
>
> *Thy word is a lamp to my feet, and a light to my path.*
>
> *Therefore I love Thy commandments above gold, yes, above fine gold.* Ps. 119:11, 92-93, 105, 127

• *Learn to confront each false belief with a specific truth from God's Word.* Once we have identified a specific false belief, we should claim God's corresponding truth in the situation. (See the chart at the end of chapter 10.)

• *Finally, take time to reflect on the marvelous biblical truths outlined in this book.* It is not the unthinking, mechanical utterance of these truths which produces freedom, but the conscious realization and application of them which changes our minds and actions. For example, when we want to affirm that we are deeply loved by God, we should think through the doctrine of propitiation; if possible, quoting 1 John 4:9-10 audibly. Through diligent study and application over a period of time, and in the context of affirming relationships, the power of God's Word will begin to conquer our false beliefs and liberate our minds.

The weapon of repentance, through rejection of false beliefs and affirmation of godly truth, has changed thousands of lives. Repentance can liberate the mind and *destroy speculations and every lofty thing raised up against the knowledge of God* (2 Cor. 10:5). And it can help us discover the wondrous significance we have in Jesus Christ: *We are deeply loved, completely forgiven, fully pleasing, totally acceptable, and complete in Him.* Our journey is a joyous and challenging adventure with Christ.

Now that we understand the value of the weapon of repentance, we will take a further look at guilt, conviction, affirmation, and faith.

Fourteen
Guilt vs. Conviction

There is no burden which produces pain, fear, and alienation quite like the feeling of guilt. Many of us know it as a constant burden. Some of us respond to it like a whipped puppy, beaten down and ashamed. Some of us avoid it through the numbing effects of denial. Our association with guilt may be prompted by many factors: poor parental modeling of Christ's love and forgiveness, divorce, neglect, a particular past sin, and the emphasis some believers place on the "ought's" and "should's" of Christianity. Regardless of these influences, guilt need not be a way of life for us.

In Rom. 8:1, Paul tells us, *There is therefore now no condemnation for those who are in Christ Jesus.* When I shared this important truth with a troubled Christian brother, his jaw dropped and his eyes filled with tears. He looked at me incredulously and exclaimed, "You mean, all this guilt I have been carrying for so long is unnecessary? I can be free from these tormenting feelings of condemnation? Why hasn't somebody told me this before?"

The Apostle Paul has been trying to tell us just that for centuries, but few of us have listened. We feel we deserve condemnation, and we fail to realize that Christ has freed us from the guilt and condemnation our sins deserve.

What exactly is guilt, anyway? Sigmund Freud said that guilt is a result of social restraint. To Freud, guilt was born in the mind of a child when his parents scolded him, and was rooted in his fear of losing the love of someone significant to him. Therefore, according to Freud, we experience guilt when we fear a loss of social esteem; when instinctive drives cause us to act in ways other than the accepted social norm.

Alfred Adler wrote that guilt arises from a refusal to accept one's inferiority. Therefore, he concluded, guilt feelings are those pangs of self-incrimination we feel anytime we think or behave inadequately.

Both Freud and Adler tried to explain the pain of guilt from a perspective that denies the righteous judgment of God and our personal responsibility for sin. To them, guilt could only be explained on a human, existential basis.

Christian authors, Bruce Narramore and Bill Counts, represent a more biblical perspective when they differentiate between true guilt and false guilt. True guilt, they explain, is an objective fact, but false guilt is a subjective feeling of pain and rejection. They emphasize that while the Bible discusses the fact of legal or theological guilt, it never tells the Christian to feel psychological guilt. These distinctions are helpful, but they may not clarify the issue for those who equate any guilt with condemnation. For this reason, we will use *guilt* and *conviction* to distinguish between the condemnation our sin deserves, and the loving motivation prompted by God to live in a way that brings honor to Him. Though many people confuse these two concepts, they are actually worlds apart. The comparisons given later in this chapter clearly illustrate their differences.

Perhaps no emotion is more destructive than guilt. It causes a loss of self-respect. It causes the human spirit to wither, and eats away at our personal significance. Guilt is a strong motivator, but it plays on our fears of failure and rejection; therefore, it can never ultimately build, encourage, or inspire us in our desire to live for Christ.

Some of us understand guilt as a sense of legal and moral accountability before God. We may try to distinguish it from low self-esteem by reasoning that guilt is the result of a sinful act or moral wrongdoing, while low self-esteem is derived from a feeling of social or personal inadequacy. Consequently, a lie makes us feel unacceptable to God and brings guilt, while bad table manners make us feel unacceptable to the people around us and bring low self-esteem.

This perspective shows some depth of thought, but it focuses on an emotional response to guilt rather than its root cause. At its root, guilt is the condition of being separated from God and of deserving condemnation for sin. Low self-esteem can be experienced by Christians or non-Christians—anyone who believes Satan's lies and feels like a failure, hopeless and rejected.

As we have determined, guilt has a restricted meaning in the New Testament. It refers only to man's condition prior to his salvation. Only the non-Christian is actually guilty before God. He has transgressed the law of God and must face the consequences. Guilt shakes its fist and says, "You have fallen short and must pay the price. You are personally accountable." Our condemnation is removed only through Christ. He took all of our guilt upon Himself when He accepted the penalty for our sins and suffered the full punishment for all sin. Because of His substitution, we need never face guilt's consequences. We are acquitted and absolved from guilt, free from our sentence of spiritual death.

Many of us have been told that we are still guilty even after we have trusted Christ to pay for our sins. And sadly, we have heard this in churches—places that should be loudly and clearly proclaiming the forgiveness and freedom found in the cross. Perhaps some people think that if they don't use guilt motivation, we won't do anything. Guilt may motivate us for a short while, until we adjust to being properly motivated. But a short period of waiting is well worth the long-term results of grace-oriented, intrinsic motivation.

Learn to identify incorrect teaching, guilt motivation, and the results of guilt in your own thoughts. Then, refuse to believe the lies any longer, and focus instead on the unconditional love and forgiveness of Christ. His love is powerful, and He is worthy of our intense zeal to obey and honor

Him. The result of proper motivation is an enduring, deepening commitment to Christ and His cause, rather than the prevalent results of guilt motivation: resentment and the desire to escape.

Christians are freed from guilt, but we are still subject to conviction. The Bible frequently speaks of the Holy Spirit's work to convict believers of sin. He directs and encourages our spiritual progress by revealing our sins in contrast to the holiness and purity of Christ.

Although the Holy Spirit convicts both believers and unbelievers of sin (John 16:8), His conviction of believers is not intended to produce pangs of guilt. Our status and self-worth are secure by the grace of God, and we are no longer guilty. Conviction deals with our behavior, not our status before God. Conviction is the Holy Spirit's way of showing the error of our performance in light of God's standard and truth. His motivation is love, correction, and protection.

While guilt is applicable to non-believers, and originates from Satan, conviction is the privilege of those who believe, and is given by the Holy Spirit. Guilt brings depression and despair, but conviction enables us to realize the beauty of God's forgiveness and to experience His love and power.

Perhaps the following will better illustrate the contrasting purposes and results of guilt and conviction:

Basic Focus:

GUILT focuses on the state of being condemned: *I am unworthy.*

CONVICTION focuses on behavior: *This act is unworthy of Christ and is destructive.*

Primary Concern:

GUILT deals with the sinner's loss of self-esteem and a wounded self-pride: *What will others think of me?*

CONVICTION deals with the loss of our moment–by–moment communication with God: *This act is destructive to me and interferes with my walk with God.*

Primary Fear:

GUILT produces a fear of punishment: *Now I'm going to get it!*

CONVICTION produces a fear of the destructiveness of the act itself: *This behavior is destructive to me and others, and it robs me of what God intends for me.*

Agent:

The agent of GUILT is Satan: *...the god of this world has blinded the minds of the unbelieving, that they might not see the light of the gospel of the glory of Christ* (2 Cor. 4:4).

The agent of CONVICTION is the Holy Spirit: *...but if by the Spirit you are putting to death the deeds of the body, you will live* (Rom. 8:13).

Behavioral Results:

GUILT leads to depression and more sin: *I am just a low-down, dirty, rotten sinner;* or to rebellion: *I don't care. I'm going to do whatever I want to do.*

CONVICTION leads to repentance, the turning from sin to Christ: *Lord, I agree with You that my sin is wrong and destructive. What do You want me to do?*

Interpersonal Result:

The interpersonal result of GUILT is alienation, a feeling of shame that drives one away from the person who has been wronged: *I can't ever face him again.*

The interpersonal result of CONVICTION is restoration, a desire to remedy the harm done to others: *Father, what would You have me do to right this wrong and restore the relationship with the one I have offended?*

Personal Results:

GUILT ends in depression, bitterness, and self-pity: *I'm just no good.*

CONVICTION ends in comfort, the realization of forgiveness:

Thank You, Lord, that I am completely forgiven and totally accepted by You!

Remedy:

The remedy for GUILT is to trust in Christ's substitutionary death to pay for the condemnation for sin.

The remedy for CONVICTION is confession, agreeing with God that our sin is wrong, that Christ has forgiven us, and that our attitude and actions will change.

Do you recognize any of your thoughts, feelings, and behaviors in these statements? Do they represent guilt or conviction?

Although Christians are no longer subject to condemnation, we will not be free from its destructive power until we learn to distinguish between guilt and conviction. The Holy Spirit wants us to be convinced that we are forgiven, accepted, and loved—totally secure—because of Christ. The Holy Spirit is the *paraclete*, or "one called along side," to lift us up and encourage us. As a part of His ministry, He faithfully makes us aware of any behavior that does not reflect the characteristics of Christ. He helps us understand both our righteousness before God and the failures in our performance.

From these observations, we can conclude that guilt is rooted in condemnation, but conviction leads us to confession and repentance, and to a renewed realization of God's grace and forgiveness.

Knowing this, how can we deal with feelings of guilt? First, we need to affirm that Christ has forgiven us and has made us judicially righteous before God. Our sin does not result in condemnation, but it is harmful and brings dishonor to God. We can confess our sin to God, claim the forgiveness we already have in Christ, and then move on in joy and freedom to honor Him. The following prayer expresses this attitude:

Father, I affirm that I am deeply loved by You, that I am fully pleasing to You, and that I am totally accepted in Your sight.

You have made me complete and have given me the
righteousness of Christ, even though my performance often
falls short. Lord, I confess my sins to You. (List them. Be
specific.) *I agree with You that these are wrong. Thank You*
for Your grace and forgiveness. Is there anything I need to
return, anyone I need to repay, or anyone I need to apologize
to? Thank You.

It is important to affirm our righteousness in Christ as well as to
confess our sins. God does not need to be reminded of our right standing
in Him, but we do. Therefore, we need to make this prayer a daily
experience and allow it to pervade our thoughts and hearts. As we yield
to the gentle prodding of God-given conviction, confess our sins, and
affirm our true relationship with Him, we will be gradually shaped and
molded in such a way that we will increasingly honor the One *who died and*
rose again on [our] behalf (2 Cor. 5:15).

We may not experience joy and freedom immediately, especially if
we have developed the painful habit of prolonged self-condemnation as a
way of dealing with sin. Loving friends who listen to us and encourage us
can be an example of God's forgiveness to us. As we become more honest
about our feelings through these affirming relationships, we will be able
to increasingly experience the freedom, forgiveness, and freshness of
God's grace.

Fifteen
The Search Concluded

As we conclude our examination of the search for significance, we will touch on several issues to help clarify how we can apply scriptural truths to our thoughts and circumstances. These issues include the contrast between our old and new nature; how we can honor Christ; how to activate our faith, and finally, how to apply the concepts in this book to our lives. First, let's see how understanding the contrast between our old and new nature can help us grow in Christ and bring honor to Him.

Our Old and New Nature

Living freely and fully in Christ requires that we put ourselves in an environment of understanding and encouragement so that we can experience God's love through His people, His Spirit, and His Word. This healthy environment will encourage us to make obedient choices, rather than follow the enticing deceptions of the world. Time after time, Scripture instructs us to exercise our wills so that we can be freed from our old way of living. As Paul taught the believers in Ephesus:

> *...in reference to your former manner of life...lay aside*
> *the old self, which is being corrupted in accordance with the*
> *lusts of deceit,*

> *and...be renewed in the spirit of your mind,*
> *and put on the new self, which in the likeness of God has*
> *been created in righteousness and holiness of the truth.*
>
> Eph. 4:22-24

In this passage, Paul explains that Christians have two natures: one which he calls the "old self" and the other, the "new self."

What exactly is the old self that must be laid aside? The *old self* is the sinful, fallen nature we possess as descendants of Adam. Scripture tells us that the old self is corrupted by the lusts of deceit (Eph. 4:22); is involved in evil practices, such as lying, slander, abusive speech, idolatry, wrath, malice, immorality, impurity, passion, evil desire, and greed (Col. 3:5, 8-9); and is a body of sin (Rom. 6:6).

In contrast, the *new self* is the nature we receive from God when we trust Christ as our Savior. This nature bears the characteristics of Christ. It has been created in the likeness of God in righteousness and holiness (Eph. 4:24), and is strengthened according to God's power through His Spirit (Eph. 3:16). The new self is a reality for all individuals born of the Spirit.

As we know, man lost his ability to reflect God's image after the Fall. Now, through faith in Jesus Christ, we are released from the domination of the natural man, and are able to put on the new self and bear His image. Although we are free from sin's absolute domination, we are not free from the influence of our old nature. Until we die and leave our physical bodies to live with Christ, our new self will continually war against our old one. Our spiritual desires will battle against our lustful, worldly desires, and our natural mind will clash with the truths of the Scriptures (Gal. 5:16-24).

Unless we are diligent, we can grow weary of spiritual warfare, and succumb to the lusts and pride in which the world delights. When we acquiesce, we adopt our old emotions and habits again. Giving in may seem attractive at the time, but sin leads to feelings of failure and low self-esteem, and it dishonors the Lord. Clearly, momentary escape from the battle isn't worth it. Sin only *appears* to be escape; actually, it is exchanging one battle in which the Holy Spirit is our powerful ally for another in which He is our loving convictor.

The more we understand biblical truth about ourselves, the better we are able to wage spiritual warfare. The Apostle Paul clearly distinguished between the character and results of the old self and the new self. His delineation in the sixth chapter of Romans centers on four words: *know, consider, present,* and *obey.* Let's examine these:

To Know

In Rom. 6:3-10, Paul instructs us to *know* the basic facts about who we are in Christ:

> *Or do you not know that all of us who have been baptized into Christ Jesus have been baptized into His death?*
>
> *Therefore we have been buried with Him through baptism into death, in order that as Christ was raised from the dead through the glory of the Father, so we too might walk in newness of life.*
>
> *For if we have become united with Him in the likeness of His death, certainly we shall be also in the likeness of His resurrection,*
>
> *knowing this, that our old self was crucified with Him, that our body of sin might be done away with, that we should no longer be slaves to sin;*
>
> *for he who has died is freed from sin.*
>
> *Now if we have died with Christ, we believe that we shall also live with Him,*
>
> *knowing that Christ, having been raised from the dead, is never to die again; death no longer is master over Him.*
>
> *For the death that He died, he died to sin, once for all; but the life He lives, He lives to God.*
>
> Rom. 6:3-10

Our old self, which deserved the condemnation of God, was identified with Christ on the cross. It was crucified with Him, and we now live, identified with Christ's resurrection *so we too might walk in newness of life*. Paul wants us to be well aware of these facts so that we can draw definite conclusions from them.

To Consider

Romans 6:11 tells us to reflect on and *consider* the facts already presented: *Even so consider yourselves to be dead to sin, but alive to God in Christ Jesus.*

To consider means "to calculate," i.e., by adding up all the facts presented in Rom. 6:1-10.[1] Unless we take the time to reflect on the implications of our identity with Christ in His death and resurrection, these most important events will be like facts learned in a history class about a battle which was fought long ago. We may be able to recite the dates, names, and places, but those facts won't make a difference in our lives. The magnificent truths of our identity in Christ deserve far more attention than our ability to repeat the facts. They deserve deep reflection on their implications in our relationships, goals, and self-esteem, both personally, and in the context of strong, healthy relationships with people who are honest, and who are growing in their personal walk with Christ.

To Present

If we understand the implications of Christ's death and resurrection (that our old self died with Christ and our new self came to life in Him), then our logical, heart-felt response will be to *present* ourselves to Him:

> *Therefore do not let sin reign in your mortal body that you should obey its lusts,*
> *and do not go on presenting the members of your body to sin as instruments of unrighteousness; but present yourselves to God as those alive from the dead, and your members as instruments of righteousness to God.* Rom. 6:12-13

We have a choice: to present the members of our bodies (our thoughts, will, goals, desires, and actions) either to sin or to God. One results in more unrighteous behavior; it is harmful to us and to others, and it dishonors God. The other results in righteous behavior, enabling us to grow, to serve, and to bring glory to God. The choice is clear, isn't it? Note that Paul doesn't start the sixth chapter of Romans with the exhortation to present ourselves to God. The commitment to action *follows* understanding the facts and considering the implications of those facts. Then, the call to commitment seems reasonable, not forced. The Lord doesn't want us to commit ourselves to something we don't understand. Commitment must follow understanding or it will be shallow, and probably, short-lived.

To Obey

After presenting ourselves to God as a reasonable response to His grace, we then need to perpetuate that commitment through moment-by-moment obedience to Him:

> *What then? Shall we sin because we are not under law but under grace? May it never be!*
>
> *Do you not know that when you present yourselves to someone as slaves for obedience, you are slaves of the one whom you obey, either of sin resulting in death, or of obedience resulting in righteousness?*
>
> *But thanks be to God that though you were slaves of sin, you became obedient from the heart to that form of teaching to which you were committed,*
>
> *and having been freed from sin, you became slaves of righteousness.*
>
> Rom. 6:15-18

Paul indicates that because we have been freed from slavery to sin, it is foolish for us to disobey. It is right and proper to obey God because our new self in Christ is now our true source of identity. He uses *slaves* to

177

signify obligation and mastery. Before we trusted Christ, we were slaves of sin, obligated to a lifestyle of unrighteousness, but now we are slaves of obedience to God, obligated to Christ, His teaching, and His righteousness.

As we identify our old selves with the fertile soil of Satan's deceptions, we will be better equipped to understand ourselves and deal properly with our ungodly thoughts, painful emotions, and unrighteous actions. Considering the old self to be dead does not mean that we deny the existence of distressing emotions. Indeed, they are very real, but now we can choose our response: either to allow them to run rampant, or to use them to identify and root out our false beliefs.

Honoring Christ

Following Christ is difficult because our culture, our old selves, and Satan fight against our desire to honor Him. Disobedience is difficult because of the painful and tragic consequences of sin. Some say that the world's way is easy; this is misleading. Others say that if we follow Christ, our lives will be free of problems, but these well-meaning people are misleading, too. We will be much better off if we realize that there is no easy way to live. Comfort is not to be our goal. Our goal, however difficult, is to honor Christ because He loves us and is worthy of our faith, love, and obedience.

But what does it mean to *honor* Christ? What can we do to bring glory to Him? Honoring Christ means accurately representing Him in every thought, action, relationship, and conversation—to bear His image. Some of the major categories of attitudes and activities that honor Christ include:

- *Love:* This love is unconditional affection for Christ, for other Christians, for unbelievers, and for ourselves. It means that we care enough to correct as well as to encourage.
- *Forgiveness:* Many of us think of forgiveness as an option, but Scripture explicitly commands us to forgive others as God through Christ has forgiven us (Matt. 18:21-35; Eph. 4:32; Col.

2:13-14). We are able to forgive more completely as we experience the Lord's forgiveness of us more deeply.

- *Holiness:* We may generally think of holiness in terms of what we don't do: abstinence from sin. But holiness also includes a positive side: zeal for Christ and His cause.
- *Biblical Values:* The more we understand the love and character of Christ, the more we will value the things that are important to Him. Prestige, money, success, and the approval of others will gradually lose their appeal, and instead, we will desire that Christ be honored, that people become Christians, that believers grow in their faith, and that missionaries be sent out to the world.
- *Giving:* Jesus said to Nicodemus, *For God so loved the world that He* gave... (John 3:16). The more we understand Him, the more we will be like Him. We have received so much from God, in both the temporal and eternal realms, that it becomes a joy to give to others in need. The measure of our lives should not be what we have, but how much we give.
- *Evangelism:* Christ has given us an example, a mission, and a command to reach others with the message of His love and forgiveness. The primary reason we don't tell more people about Him is because we fear their rejection, but His acceptance of us transcends the disapproval of others. The world (including our neighbors) desperately needs to hear a clear, loving presentation of the gospel. It is our privilege as His chosen ambassadors to share it with them.
- *Discipleship:* Christ discipled the people around Him by His example and by communicating truth to them. His love, humility, strength, and tenderness provided a powerful context for learning. If we want others to grow in their faith, we need to follow His example and model the life we study and teach.
- *Social Activism:* The influence of Christ should not be relegated only to the spiritual aspect of life. In the last century, William Wilburforce led the struggle against slavery in England, basing

his arguments squarely on the Scriptures. In civil rights, politics, abortion, education, and in every other area of life, Christ is the source of truth, justice, and love. It is our privilege and our responsibility to represent Him in all aspects of our culture.

- *Prayer:* Christ said, *Apart from Me, you can do nothing* (John 15:5). Our programs and activities are unproductive in the eternal sense if we do not base them on the Word of Christ and accomplish them according to the power of Christ. Prayer reflects our dependence on Him.

- *Worship:* Perhaps our greatest expression of love for God is worship—speaking and/or singing of His greatness. Whether we worship on Sunday morning with hundreds of others, or alone, this expression properly reflects dependence, thankfulness, and praise.

Glorifying God is not limited to any given time or place. It is our privilege at every moment to accurately reflect our Creator and Savior to others, to ourselves, and to Him. Why? Because He rightly deserves it. As the following scene in heaven vividly illustrates, Christ is worthy of our praise and obedience:

> *And I looked, and I heard the voice of many angels around the throne and the living creatures and the elders; and the number of them was myriads of myriads, and thousands of thousands,*
>
> *saying with a loud voice, "Worthy is the Lamb that was slain to receive power and riches and wisdom and might and honor and glory and blessing."*
>
> *And every created thing which is in heaven and on the earth and under the earth and on the sea, and all things in them, I heard saying, "To Him who sits on the throne, and to the Lamb, be blessing and honor and glory and dominion forever and ever."*

*And the four living creatures kept saying, "Amen." And
the elders fell down and worshiped.*

Rev. 5:11-14

Activating Our Faith

Throughout this book, we have seen how sin plunged man into
spiritual darkness and how that darkness has blinded his eyes to truth. We
have seen how every individual born in sin has been deceived by false
beliefs, resulting in improper thoughts, emotions, and actions. Through
this veil of darkness, it is impossible for the sinful man to earn the love and
acceptance of God.

But in this darkness, we have discovered a light as God Himself has
provided a path to an intimate relationship with Him. That light is Jesus
Christ, from whom we freely receive salvation, forgiveness, justification,
propitiation, and acceptance. By faith, in a miraculous instant, we have
been adopted into a new family, have received an inheritance as sons and
daughters of God, and have been given the purpose of representing the
Lord to those around us. We can devote the rest of our lives to understanding
and experiencing these incredible truths.

We have seen that our relationship with God, our security, and our
self-worth are not earned by our efforts. They are obtained only by faith.
This point is so important, let's take some time to analyze what faith is.

Faith has several synonyms: *trust, dependence, reliance,* and *belief.*
The focus is on the object of faith, not the faith itself. For example, if I
believe that a certain chair will hold me when I sit in it, the primary issue
is the construction and quality of the chair—the *object* of my faith, not the
amount of faith I have. Even if I believe very strongly that the chair will
support me, if the chair is a rotten, broken-down piece of junk, then it will
break if I try to sit in it. My faith will not make it a good chair. But if the
chair is of quality construction, it takes very little faith to sit comfortably
in it. Again, it is the quality of the object, not the quantity of my faith, that
is of primary importance.

In Christianity, Christ is the object of faith, and faith is our trust in in His character and abilities. The more we know Him, the more we will trust Him. Faith, then, requires our knowing God, and knowing Him requires a relationship. To know God, we need to talk to Him through prayer, listen to His voice, see Him at work in our lives and the lives of others, and search out His will and deeds through the Scriptures He has given us. *So faith comes by hearing, and hearing by the word of Christ* (Rom. 10:17).

Make no mistake about it, faith is not a magic formula for manipulating God to grant us the wishes of our hearts. We cannot motivate God to act contrary to His sovereign will. Faith enables us to be partakers with Him, to gain wisdom from Him, and to bring His love and power to bear on human situations with lasting impact.

Let me explain it this way. Suppose Rusty needs $1,000 by Saturday to pay off an important obligation. Today is Wednesday, and Rusty has yet to raise the money.

Rusty decides to call John, a trusted friend. John is more than happy to supply the need, but tells Rusty to wait until Saturday, the very day the money is due. "Give me until Saturday," John says. "I'll have the money for you by noon."

Rusty can relax, realizing that his need has been met. Although he has yet to actually see the money, he has confidence in his close friend. After all, John has always been reliable, and is a person of means. If he says he wants to help meet Rusty's need and will supply the $1,000, certainly he will do so. Knowing that, Rusty can wait patiently until Saturday without anxiety. He has faith that John can and will deliver as promised because he has an intimate knowledge of John's proven character and ability.

Likewise, our faith in God lies in what we know of His character and ability. His character is one of love, revealed to us as a benevolent Father who desires to bestow good gifts to His children. And yet, a good Father knows that not all of the requests of His children are beneficial to them; therefore, some of them cannot be granted.

We often find situations in life when we want something that seems very good and reasonable to us, but either God's Word opposes it, or our prayers seem fruitless. There are at least three questions we must ask in these situations:

- *Is it God's will?* Do the Scriptures prohibit it, allow it, or promise it?
- *Is it for God's glory?* What is our motive: pleasure, prestige, or to honor Christ?
- *Is it in God's timing?* Are there conditions to be met? Does He want us to wait?

It is then that we must exercise our faith to trust in His character alone, even without visible evidence to support our trust. As the psalmist wrote:

> *I would have despaired unless I had believed that I would see the goodness of the Lord in the land of the living.*
> *Wait for the Lord; be strong, and let your heart take courage; yes, wait for the Lord.*
>
> Ps. 27:13-14

When we know God and realize from His Word that He is both powerful and compassionate, we can then trust in Him despite what our feelings or human perceptions tell us.

Too often, however, we presume upon the will of God by rationalizing that what we are asking is beneficial for us. We think that God should be more than willing to grant our request; however, we must remember that God sees a bigger picture than we do. He can see the future, other relating circumstances, and all of the events that will affect our lives. Though we may ask a specific request according to His will, we must not despair if we do not see an immediate response. And we must remember that a creative God can take all of His children's best interests in interrelated events and resolve the matter in a way we least expect. God's timing and methods are a mystery, and require our faith in His love and sovereignty:

> *Oh, the depth of the riches both of the wisdom and knowledge of God! How unsearchable are His judgments and unfathomable His ways!*
>
> Rom. 11:33

We need to dispel another common misunderstanding about faith. Some people believe that true faith exists only in the absence of doubt, but this is not necessarily the case. Biblical faith often exists in spite of our doubts. If we think that we need to be freed of conflicting thoughts and emotions for our faith to be honoring to the Lord, we will become introspective and be disappointed. Conflicting thoughts and emotions will be a normal part of our lives until we go to be with the Lord. Learn to be honest in conflict rather than deny its existence.

The account of Abraham and Isaac is an example of God-honoring faith in spite of doubts and conflicting emotions. In Gen. 12:1-3 and 17:1-5, God established and repeated a solemn covenant with Abraham which included the promise to *make [him] the father of a multitude of nations* (Gen. 17:5).

It probably didn't take Abraham long to figure out that if he was to be the father of many nations, he would have to have at least one child! When he was eighty-six years old and Sarah, his wife, was seventy-six years old, Abraham had his first child, but there was a problem. This child was not Sarah's. It was the child of Hagar, Sarah's maid. God indicated that the child, Ishmael, wasn't exactly what He had in mind as the first heir of the father of many nations. So, after fourteen long years, Abraham and Sarah (now 100 years old and ninety years old, respectively) miraculously had a son, Isaac. You can imagine how happy they were that God had given them this boy, the answer to His promise, when they were so far beyond the childbearing age!

But God was not through with Abraham. The twenty-second chapter of Genesis records God's command to him:

> *Now it came about after these things, that God tested Abraham, and said to him, "Abraham!" And he said, "Here I am."*
>
> *And He said, "Take now your son, your only son, whom you love, Isaac, and go to the land of Moriah; and offer him there as a burnt offering on one of the mountains of which I will tell you."*
>
> Gen. 22:1-2

Do you think Abraham had some conflicting thoughts and emotions? The miracle-child, the first-born son, the heir to the promise of God to be sacrificed as a burnt offering? We get a glimpse of the reasoning of Abraham's heart in the following verses:

> *So Abraham rose early in the morning and saddled his donkey, and took two of his young men with him and Isaac his son; and he split wood for the burnt offering, and arose and went to the place of which God had told him.*
>
> *On the third day Abraham raised his eyes and saw the place from a distance.*
>
> *And Abraham said to his young men, "Stay here with the donkey, and I and the lad will go yonder; and we will worship and return to you."*
>
> Gen. 22:3-5

"*We* will worship and return to you," Abraham said. Hebrews 11:19 states that Abraham *considered that God is able to raise men even from the dead.* Yes, Abraham would kill his only son if that was what God required, but God surely would raise Isaac from the dead so that His promise would not be broken.

As it turned out, God stopped Abraham from killing Isaac, and Isaac did not have to be raised from the dead. But there is an important point for us to learn about dealing with conflicting thoughts and emotions: We need to act on the revealed will of God as explained in the Scriptures, and focus on His love, promises, and power. Abraham did not focus on his conflicting thoughts and emotions, though he probably had many. Nor did he deny having them; rather, he simply didn't let them determine his actions. The promise of God to provide an heir and the command of God to kill Isaac looked mutually exclusive, but the sovereign Almighty God is able to accomplish far more than we can understand. We can have faith in His greatness, wisdom, and love, even when we don't understand what He is doing.

Application

Christ, His Word, and His work to accomplish our redemption are worthy of our faith. At this point you may be wondering, *How do I start applying these principles?*

First, you need to understand the four truths of redemption and the four corresponding false beliefs that we often mistake for truth. The ability to understand truth and recognize deception is a vital first step.

Secondly, learn to reject lies and replace them with their biblical truths so that your mind will be in the process of renewal. Along with renewing your mind, look for opportunities to represent Christ accurately and actively in your every situation and relationship. *The Search for Significance Workbook* has been developed to help you apply these truths so that your self-concept, your ambitions, and your relationships will begin to reflect the character of Christ.

Then, third, teach these truths to others. Teaching is the best way to learn because we pay more attention and study more diligently when we are going to communicate scriptural truths to someone else.

And fourth, endure. Develop a godly tenacity and keep following Christ. You will make mistakes, someone may disapprove of you, you may blame someone, you may sometimes fail to apply these truths, and you will occasionally dishonor the Lord, but realize that you are *deeply loved, completely forgiven, fully pleasing, totally accepted, and complete* because Christ died for you and was raised from the dead to give you new life. You are free! Free to *proclaim the excellencies of Him who has called you out of darkness into His marvelous light* (1 Pet. 2:9).

Notes

Chapter 7. Approval Addict

1. Lori Thorkelson Rentzel, *Emotional Dependency* (San Rafael, CA: Exodus International-North America, Box 2121, 94912.

2. C.S. Lewis, *The Four Loves* (New York: Harcourt Brace Jovanovich, Inc., 1960), pp. 91-92.

3. Lori Thorkelson Rentzel, *Emotional Dependency*, pp. 3-4. Reprinted by permission.

Chapter 9. Shame

1. Louis Berkhof, *Systematic Theology* (Grand Rapids, MI: William B. Eerdmans Pub. Co., 1941), p. 468.

Chapter 15. The Search Concluded

1. Ryrie, Charles C., Th.D., Ph.D., *The Ryrie Study Bible*, New American Standard Translation (Chicago, IL: Moody Press, 1976, 1978), p. 1710, s.v. "consider," v. 6:11.

Rapha

Christ-Centered Hospital and Counseling Care

*D*ear Friend,

In my heart, I feel that many people who read this book will be suffering from serious emotional or substance abuse problems or they will know someone who is. If so, I want them to know that there's hope.

You might be suffering yourself. And if you are, I want to assure you that there's hope for you, too, regardless of how serious your problems might be.

Our organization, RAPHA, provides Christ-centered treatment in hospitals and other settings where caring, committed professionals are seeing people of all ages healed of some of the most severe problems imaginable. The success stories we hear from children, youth and adults are indeed thrilling.

I want to encourage you to read the following pages very carefully. You will find information that will answer questions you might have about RAPHA and tell you more about the wide range of services we offer.

If you, personally, need help, or if you want to help someone, give us a call at 1-800-227-2657. Your inquiry will be strictly confidential.

Remember, we're here to serve you and to offer hope.

In Christ,

Robert S. McGee

Robert S. McGee
President

"It has been good to know that we now have a place to refer persons we counsel who are in need of hospital care for emotional, spiritual and substance abuse problems."

Dr. Jerry Falwell
Pastor, Thomas Road Baptist Church
Founder, Old-Time Gospel Hour
Chancellor, Liberty University
Lynchburg, Virginia

"For years our churches have needed an anointed referral center to minister to those whose needs lie beyond the church counseling center. RAPHA is the answer."

Dr. Jimmy Draper
Pastor, First Baptist Church
Euless, Texas
Past President of the Southern Baptist
Convention

"*S*urely the ministry of RAPHA has been blessed by God! Christians everywhere should rejoice that there is such a program available in this country!"

T. W. Wilson
Associate to Billy Graham
Billy Graham Evangelistic Association

"*I* appreciate the commitment that RAPHA has for the American teenager. RAPHA's treatment program comes from a biblical perspective and has brought about true healing for emotional needs."

Dawson McAllister
President, Shepherd Productions
Irving, Texas

"RAPHA is an excellent balance of clinical and spiritual. They are treating needs in a unique and dynamic way."

Ben Kinchlow
Author/Speaker

"There has been a great need for treatment with a sound spiritual perspective. RAPHA offers that kind of program."

Pat Boone
Actor, Singer, Author and Chairman of the National Easter Seal Society

"RAPHA is committed to healing broken lives. I give it my heartiest endorsement and pray that God will use this ministry significantly."

Dr. Lewis A. Drummond
President, Southeastern Baptist Theological Seminary
Wake Forest, North Carolina

"I have longed for a Christ-centered ministry that addresses problems without sacrificing biblical principles. I believe RAPHA is such a program."

Dr. Adrian Rogers
Pastor, Bellevue Baptist Church
Memphis, Tennessee
Past President of the Southern Baptist Convention

True stories of God's miracles through RAPHA

Depression

"After 21 years of depression and having been on several types of treatment units, I am at last finally free from depression. The RAPHA unit is a place where you can meet God face-to-face."

"I was about as far down as I could go. I thank RAPHA for its support, concern and patience. Thanks for lifting me up to higher ground!"

"I truly thank our wonderful Lord for RAPHA. I've been feeling just great! I have suddenly noticed the beautiful world around me and look up toward heaven to thank the Lord for the beautiful trees and grass and the singing birds. For so long—three years—while I was going through depression I never noticed the beauty around me! Isn't God great?"

RAPHA ministers to adults and adolescents.

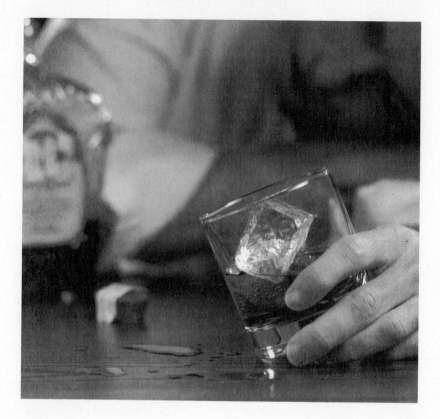

Chemical Dependency

RAPHA has taught me so much. I'm not preaching to my friends that use drugs; I'm just being an example of how you can deal with your problems instead of using drugs as an escape."

"The RAPHA program is great! I'm doing so well and have had no trouble staying away from drugs."

"We want to express our appreciation to you for all the help you have given our family resulting in the admission of our son to your facility and for helping him to overcome his alcohol addiction."

Eating Disorders

*"For over 17 years I had bulimia
and was ready to take my life. If it
were not for RAPHA, I would still
have this terrible eating disorder.
I'm a changed person; I'm a
confident person with more
self-esteem than I've ever had with
a good positive attitude about life.
I now realize that God loves me
deeply, completely forgives me,
that I'm fully pleasing to Him,
totally acceptable to Him, and am
complete in Christ. I like me. I
now understand that I don't need
to earn love, that I'm worthy to be
loved, just as I am for who I am."*

**RAPHA provides general
psychiatric and substance
abuse treatment.**

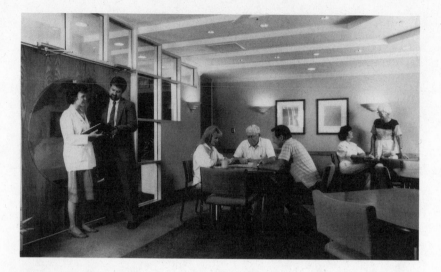

Other Disorders

- Suicidal and/or homicidal ideations or attempts
- Noticeable negative changes in behavior
- Poor impulse control (stealing, aggression, etc.)
- Violent outbursts toward others
- Progressive or extreme withdrawal
- Disordered, unmanageable behaviors
- Imminent failure of social, familial, or occupational functioning
- Mania
- Psychosis
- Paranoia, phobias
- Periods of confusion
- Severe loss of memory
- Delusional systems (hallucinations)
- Uncontrollably obsessive thoughts
- Anxiety attacks
- Multiple personality manifestations
- Impairment of thoughts, judgment, logic or reality testing
- Inability to carry out activities of daily living

Call RAPHA
Toll Free, 24 hours a day
1-800-227-2657

Confidentiality <u>is</u> guaranteed.

What happens when you call RAPHA?

1. Evaluation will be made to determine if the person would benefit from one of RAPHA's programs.

2. The various treatment programs will be explained.

3. Financial aid and insurance availability will be explained.

4. If one of our programs is selected, admissions issues will be worked out prior to arrival at the treatment location. This includes travel aid, if needed.